Critical Guides to Spanish Texts

24 García Lorca: Poeta en Nueva York

Critical Guides to Spanish Texts

EDITED BY J. E. VAREY AND A. D. DEYERMOND

FEDERICO GARCÍA LORCA

Poeta en Nueva York

Derek Harris

Lecturer in Spanish,
University College, London

Grant & Cutler Ltd *in association with*
Tamesis Books Ltd 1978

© Grant & Cutler Ltd
   1978
ISBN   0 7293 0066 8

I.S.B.N. 84-499-2457-X
DEPÓSITO LEGAL: V. 252 - 1979

Printed in Spain by
Artes Gráficas Soler, S.A., Valencia
for
GRANT AND CUTLER LTD
11, BUCKINGHAM STREET, LONDON, W.C.2

Contents

Contents

Preface

A guide to Lorca's *Poeta en Nueva York* encounters an immediate problem. The book was published after his death and the typescript from which it was prepared has in large part disappeared. There is no guarantee that the text we have corresponds to the contents and structure intended by Lorca, although it does seem likely that it is not substantially different from what he intended. A further problem is the difficulty of the poems.

Poeta en Nueva York was very different from the popular song poems with which Lorca made his reputation in the 1920s. The response of many readers and critics to the change of style in this book was puzzlement and hostility. This attitude is continued in many early monographs on Lorca which give only scant and cursory reference to *Poeta en Nueva York*. The first critics to give serious consideration to the book were Angel del Río and Gustavo Correa in the 1950s (*29* and *32*).[†] In 1962 an enormous contribution to the detailed study of the poems was made by C. Marcilly (*24* and *25*). Recently there have been very important discoveries concerning the textual problems and the biographical background to the book (*5-10*). The increase of critical interest in *Poeta en Nueva York* can be judged by the recent appearance of two short monographs (*18* and *26*).

The approach taken by this guide will be to follow, by and large, the order of the poems as they appear in the book, and in view of their difficulty, to analyse, as far as possible, poems as a whole. The analysis will focus in particular on the system of symbols Lorca uses. The commentary will contain frequent references to traditional symbols. The sources for such references are: *Brewers Dictionary of Phrase and Fable* (London: Cassell, 1974), *Hall's Dictionary of Subjects and Symbols in Art* (London: John Murray, 1974), J. E. Cirlot, *A Dictionary of Symbols* (London: Routledge and Kegan Paul, 1976),

---

[†]References to works listed in the Bibliographical Note are indicated by a numeral in italics, followed where necessary by a page number.

J. A. Pérez-Rioja, *Diccionario de símbolos y mitos* (Madrid: Tecnos, 1962). In the interest of avoiding excessive and complicated notes I shall not give specific references to such sources.

Quotations from *Poeta en Nueva York* will be from the best text available at the moment, that included in the nineteenth edition of Lorca's *Obras completas* (Madrid: Aguilar, 1974). I shall refer to the poems by stanza number and line number, so that any text of the poems may be used in conjunction with this guide. I shall avoid any discussion of the book's textual problems, which would occupy much of the space needed for commentary on the poems themselves. To avoid even more complication I shall not refer to variants in manuscripts or earlier published versions of the poems.

Chapters IV and V of this guide incorporate arguments developed previously in an article in the *Bulletin of Hispanic Studies* (*21*). Part of the argument in the first chapter has also been previously published in *Insula* (*20*). I should like to thank the editors of both periodicals for their permission to incorporate this material. I should also like to express my gratitude to the editors of this series, Professors Deyermond and Varey, for their meticulous care and help during the preparation of this guide. I am especially grateful to Professor Varey for all that I learned from 1964 to 1966 while attending the seminar on *Poeta en Nueva York* organised by him at Westfield College.

I Lorca and Surrealism

Lorca was a poet of singular intensity focussed sharply on a narrow range of themes. His work is a cockpit for a struggle between life and death, love and sterility. The conflict makes him a dramatic poet, and the unequal stature of the combatants makes him a tragic poet. Life is weak and defenceless, pursued relentlessly by a malignant death-force. Love too is often powerless in the presence of an all-pervading sterility. Yet in the midst of death Lorca asserts the value of life, and in the midst of sterility he proclaims the power of sexuality. Not triumphantly, for the victory of love and life is improbable, but because of a commitment to the values of life against those of death.

He is best known for the poems that use the forms and techniques of popular song, poems in which he develops the dramatic intensity so characteristic of his work and also a personal system of symbols representing the two sides in the conflict of life and death. The moon and the knife, for example, are images and agents of death, while the sun and the horse are the images and agents of life. Lorca's poetry in the popular manner culminated in the immediate and immense success of his collection of ballads, the *Romancero gitano*, published in 1928. Instead of then continuing to write in the same vein he began to experiment, with long poems on abstract themes and with prose poems in a markedly avant-garde style. And then he went to New York.

In the summer of 1928 Lorca was beset by what an acquaintance of the time later described as a "penumbra sentimental" (*4*, p.72), an emotional crisis whose causes were many and complex, and which moreover can only be a matter of conjecture. Some of Lorca's letters from this period show him in a state of deep depression (*1*, II, p.1232-6). The visit to New York, with the pretext of enrolling at Columbia University to learn English, was in fact a form of therapy to lift the shadow of depression. Something of his state of mind can be gained from a letter written on board the ship taking him to America: "No sé para qué he partido; me lo pregunto cien veces al día. Me miro en

el espejo del estrecho camarote y no me reconozco. Parezco otro
Federico . . ." (*1*, II, p.1239). Here is more than a suggestion that
the "penumbra sentimental", whatever its causes, had provoked a
crisis of identity. The poems written in America would seem to
support the suggestion.

Lorca arrived in New York in the last week of June 1929. In mid-
August he left the city to spend a month or so in the countryside of
Vermont, first at Eden Mills then at Shandaken. Letters written
after his return to New York in September seem to show him in a
happier frame of mind, at peace with himself and, apparently, with
his new environment (*1*, II, pp.1115-16). However, at the beginning
of October he withdrew from his English classes, possibly a sign that
his adaptation to the new environment had ended. Some of the most
violent and bitter of the New York poems date from the autumn and
winter of 1929-30. He later claimed to be greatly impressed by the
stock market collapse in October 1929 (*1*, I, p.1099), although some
of the poems predate the Black Monday of October 29th. But if
Lorca had experienced a revival of his personal depression, the stock
market collapse could well have appeared to him as the collapse of
the American Dream, reflecting the tottering state of his inner world.

Nonetheless his last six months in New York were filled with a
busy round of social engagements, lectures and dinners. In March
1930 he left for Cuba where he had been invited to give a series of
lectures. His stay on the island seems to have been a happy one, a
renewal of old acquaintances and the making of many new ones in a
return to a Hispanic ambience. In mid-June he set sail for Cadiz.

Poeta en Nueva York is a carefully structured book. The poems are
not in strict chronological order of composition but arranged in ten
titled sections that follow the biographical pattern of Lorca's stay in
America. The book is a record of a violent personal alienation in a
horrific urban environment, an account of pain and anguish in a
dehumanised world where materialism crushes all spirituality. A
religious concern is a particularly distinctive theme. The book is
mainly a collection of fairly long poems in free verse, in a style that
has frequently been described as surrealist. In view of the difficulty of
interpreting these poems this opening chapter will concern itself with
examining the nature of their expression.

The most common definition of surrealism as the use in art and literature of material from dreams and the subconscious gives an inadequate description of the surrealist movement. The movement was centred on Paris and the principle theoreticians and practitioners were French, at least as far as literary practice was concerned. The French surrealists had inherited many of the nihilistic attitudes of the avant-garde around the time of the Great War, especially of the anti-art movement Dada. They proffered violent and deliberate insults to art, society, state and religion. They wanted to smash the restrictions, inhibitions and artificiality of what they saw as the unreal world of middle-class convention.

What the surrealists wanted to achieve was the state of mind they called surreality, which may be defined as a condition where all divisions between the conscious and the subconscious are removed. For the literary surrealists the method of achieving the state of surreality was, at least initially, automatic writing, writing produced in a trance-like condition in which expression is released from the normal procedures of order and selection exercised by rational, aesthetic and moral judgement. However, automatic writing is merely a technique for suppressing controlling mechanisms. The defining principle of surrealism is the attempt to give free expression to the subconscious, by whatever means.

By the second half of the 1920s the activities of the French surrealists were becoming well known in literary and artistic circles in Spain (*37*, pp.12-21). In 1928 and 1929 books by major poets, Rafael Alberti, Vicente Aleixandre and Luis Cernuda, show symptoms of an awareness of French surrealism. These poets exploited surrealist themes and techniques to help them express deeply disturbing personal crises which happened to coincide with the political crisis in Spain in the late 1920s. The disintegrating social and political situation of Spain found a parallel in the break-up of the poets' inner world of dreams and illusions.

The violence of this emotional disturbance produced feelings too wild and bewildered to be filtered through the normal rational processes of creative writing. This situation helped to establish a ready sympathy for the suppression of intellectual control proposed by the surrealists, and an even readier sympathy for their mystique of rebellion. In the Spanish poets rational, aesthetic and moral barriers were brushed aside by violent emotions seeking urgent expression, with the result that they rarely, if ever, need to employ the contrived technique of automatism to free their expression from conscious control. This produces a poetry with a more consistent emotional tenor than is often found in French surrealism and a greater coherence in the use of imagery.

A number of Spanish poets at this time seem to have found themselves in a state of hypersensitivity in which trivial objects and phenomena acquired extraordinary and violent emotional significance. Their vision becomes almost hallucinatory, an experience that was not unknown to some French surrealists, notably Louis Aragon and Robert Desnos. The vision that sees strange significance in innocent objects can be linked closely with the concept of the objective correlative. An objective correlative is an event or object that evokes an emotional experience without having any apparent logical relationship with the experience. Moreover, when the objective correlative is used as a literary device it creates a mode of expression in which intensity is gained at the expense of clarity.[1] Now the Spanish poets, in a state of emotional disturbance, were unable to express themselves with clarity, yet at the same time they had a great need to convey the intensity of their feelings.

The combination of hallucinatory experience with the expressive technique of the objective correlative may be regarded as what produces poetry of a surrealist nature in Spain. A heightened and distorted perception enables the Spanish poets to use private symbols and imagery created by processes of free association in a way that has the lack of inhibition of French surrealism but which retains a measure of control derived from the emotional condition they seek to express.

Lorca's attitude to surrealism was equivocal. First evidence of his awareness of the movement appears in a lecture given in Granada in 1928 in which he discusses the element of autonomy in the poetic practice of the 1920s. The way in which a poem tended to become a self-sufficient entity without reference to any reality outside itself is defined by him as an evasion of reality, and surrealism is used as

---

[1] For a fuller discussion of the elements of hallucination and the objective correlative in the context of Spanish surrealism see Derek Harris, *Luis Cernuda: A Study of the Poetry* (London: Tamesis Books, 1973), pp.34-6.

an example of this:

> Esta evasión poética puede hacerse de muchas maneras. El surrealismo emplea el sueño y su lógica para escapar. En el mundo de los sueños, el realísimo mundo de los sueños, se encuentran indudablemente normas poéticas de emoción verdadera. Pero esta evasión por medio del sueño o del subconsciente es, aunque muy pura, poco diáfana. Los latinos queremos perfiles y misterio visible. Forma y sensualidades. (*1*, I, pp.1039-40)

While not antagonistic to surrealism this statement has the specific aim of differentiating it from Lorca's own poetic practice. In the summer of 1928 he sent to the Catalan critic Sebastián Gasch two prose poems, describing them in the following way:

> Responden a mi nueva manera *espiritualista*. emoción pura descarnada, desligada del control lógico, pero, ¡ojo!, ¡ojo!, con una tremenda lógica poética. No es surrealismo, ¡ojo!, la conciencia más clara los ilumina. (*1*, II, p.1219)

Here is an even greater reluctance to be associated with surrealism. However, the reference to "la conciencia más clara" indicates an equation in Lorca's mind between surrealism and automatism, and it may well be automatism from which he really wished to dissociate himself. The freedom from logical control, which he admits, would certainly bring him near to surrealism's orbit, and critical comment has noted the surrealist appearance of these prose poems (*24*, p.52).

Evidence of a possible surrealist element in Lorca's writings can be found in the plays *Así que pasen cinco años* and *El público*, both dating at least in part from his stay in New York and Cuba, and in particular in the film script he wrote in New York in collaboration with the Mexican artist Emilio Amero. Amero recalls that Lorca talked to him about *Un Chien andalou*, and the script itself bears a strong affinity with Buñuel's film (*2*, p.34). As far as *Poeta en Nueva York* is concerned most of the critics who have noted a surrealist quality in the poems have added careful qualifications. Thus Guillermo Díaz-Plaja in 1932 referred to Lorca's "superrealismo personalísimo" in which "las palabras conservan toda su fuerza plástica, cromática, viva, y sugieren realidades de bulto, inmediatas, dramáticamente y por imágenes muy sencillas" (*19*, p.3). Here is an elaboration of the poet's own expressed preference for "perfiles y misterio visible". A later critic, Carlos Ramos-Gil, has declared that while *Poeta en Nueva York* cannot be considered a completely surrealist work, the use of free association and symbolism unrestrained by logic is evidence of surrealist influence. He speaks of a "surrealismo controlado" in which there is a conscious control of subconscious material (*40*, p.160). This idea is an alternative statement of Lorca's own concept of a governing "lógica poética".

The use of free association and the apparent irrationality of images is in Lorca the product of the state of hypersensitivity and quasihallucinatory vision referred to earlier. Virginia Higginbotham has spoken of a "heightened perception of disorder and chaos" in connection with the New York poems (*22*, p.116). Carlos Edmundo de Ory has specifically declared that Lorca saw the city in a state of genuine hallucination (*39*, p.116). This distorted, dislocated vision creates images that are the product of mechanisms outside rational control, but such images are subject to an alternative control, the "tremenda lógica poética". Lorca exploits the surrealist freedom from moral, aesthetic or rational constraint, but only as a means of production for his imagery. He does not seek to establish the condition of surreality where conscious and subconscious experience combine.

The element of control and the links with the concrete reality of the city in the imagery of *Poeta en Nueva York* have been described with remarkable insight by Gustavo Correa, who refers to the process of ordering of the imagery as the production of a system of negative and positive symbols (*32*, p.167). Such a system is a basic characteristic of all of Lorca's work, but it becomes more complex in *Poeta en Nueva York* and provides a key to the understanding of these poems. The existence of identifiable negative and positive symbols indicates another essential quality of the American poems: they possess an ethical dimension. This is an additional factor differentiating Lorca's practice from the French mode of surrealism, and its presence in the poems raises the possibility of a further influence, that of expressionism.

Expressionism, strictly speaking, is the equivalent in German art and literature of the avant-garde activity in other European countries, especially cubism, fauvism and futurism. Several commentaries on German expressionism, and even some translations of German expressionist poetry, appeared in Spanish literary periodicals in 1920-2. Expressionism also has the general meaning of a violent artistic distortion directed at the communication of an intense emotion; an example in Spanish literature would be the *esperpentos* of Valle-Inclán. *Poeta en Nueva York* has in fact been compared with the poetry of Wildgans and Trakl (*41*, pp.248-9), and with the paintings of Ensor, Nolde and Klein (*34*, pp.287-8). Carlos Edmundo de Ory has spoken of "an expressionistic type of Spanish surrealism" (*39*, p.98). Expressionism is characterised not only by its emotional violence but also by its political commitment and utopianism. I do not wish to suggest even remotely an influence of German expressionism on Lorca, but the view of man and society put forward in *Poeta en Nueva York* does have undoubted general expressionist qualities, in particular distortion, emotionalism, political awareness and a reformist criticism of society. One might perhaps conclude that the book is an amalgam of surrealist techniques and expressionist themes.

The difficulty of *Poeta en Nueva York* lies in its imagery, whose nature I shall now examine more closely. A basic theme of the book is a conflict of values, and this, with its associated ethical judgements, produces the arrangement of the imagery into positive and negative symbols. The image-creating process, however, can vary widely from the completely traditional to an extreme illogicality that has all the airs of surrealism.

The ethical image system relies heavily on traditional sources. Light and darkness, day and night, for example, are used to express the conflict of values, as are images drawn from nature and contrasted with those of the new urban environment. *Poeta en Nueva York* also includes a number of the symbols established in Lorca's earlier poems, such as the death symbol of the moon. But the New York poems add to the system many symbols not used before; indeed there is a whole range of vocabulary entirely peculiar to these poems. Usually they are straight one-for-one symbols: cancer=death, ferns=childhood. An idiosyncratic feature is the presence of tropical, often African, animals in the city.

The conflict of positive and negative forces is frequently given form by the technique of paradox, especially as paradox between a noun and an adjective. An adjective is used to negate the positive quality of a noun. A particularly striking sequence of such usage occurs with the noun "cielo":

cielo vacío . . . cielo mondado . . . cielo barrido . . . cielo solo . . .
cielo desierto . . . cielo extraño . . . cielo duro . . . cielo triste . . .

cielo sin salida . . . cielos yertos en declive . . . cielos amarillos . . .
cielos hechos añicos.

This list is by no means exhaustive. Destructive adjectivisation may
be taken as a basic characteristic of these poems.

The technique of the transferred epithet is frequently employed,
and may be quite complex as in the following example, from the
book's opening poem, where the transferred epithets are both
destructive and also part of a process of personification: "el agua
harapienta de los pies secos." Water, a natural life-force, is personified by "harapienta", which negates the positive associations of water,
making the water an image of suffering and mutilation. Personification
enables the water to have feet. That these feet should be dry is a
paradox, a negation of the positive, wet nature of water. "Pies secos"
also evokes an immediate reminiscence of "pies desnudos", and
associations of suffering linked with "harapienta". The switching
of adjectives and the personification produce a highly compressed
image of great emotional intensity. An apparently illogical image is
the product of a quite rational, and traditional, process of elaboration.
Yet the unusual intensity and compression with which traditional
image-building techniques are used creates the appearance of a self-
sufficient, "surrealist" image. Moreover it would seem that it was
Lorca's intention to create such an appearance. The image has been
subjected to a deliberate process of distortion in order to inhibit a
rational comprehension and to promote an emotional intensity that
seeks a primarily emotional comprehension. This is a case of Lorca's
"tremenda lógica poética".

The use of traditional techniques is one of the ways in which the
freely associative imagery in the New York poems is controlled.
Correa has pointed out how symbols are also used as controlling
devices. A remarkable feature of *Poeta en Nueva York* is the use of
allusion, and even direct reference, to classical mythology, something
quite unexpected in a Spanish writer of the late 1920s and in a
surrealist-influenced text. Such classical allusion cannot therefore
be casual. Lorca names four classical deities: Jupiter, Diana, Apollo
and Saturn. Apollo is used as a symbol of masculine beauty in "Tu
infancia en Mentón" and "Oda a Walt Whitman", and in his classical
role as the representative of rational, civilised behaviour in contrast
to the free celebration of sexuality associated with Dionysus. Jupiter

appears in "Fábula y rueda de los tres amigos" in what seems to be the function of God the Father, in this case negated. In "Tu infancia en Mentón" Saturn is presented in his traditional role of god of seed-time, while, strangely, he stops trains running in "Poema doble del lago Edem", an action that perhaps alludes to the malevolence of Saturn as a synonym for Chronos. That classical allusion is not simply gratuitous can be seem in the reference to Diana in "Fábula y rueda de los tres amigos":

> Diana es dura,
> pero a veces tiene los pechos nublados.
> Puede la piedra blanca latir en la sangre del ciervo
> y el ciervo puede soñar por los ojos de un caballo.

Diana, the goddess of the moon, that standard Lorcan death symbol, was a virgin and also the goddess of chastity, the female counterpart of Apollo and the enemy of Venus. Her association with the moon enables her to have clouded breasts, and also provides a secondary meaning for the adjective "dura". The clouded breasts have a concessive relationship with the moon, suggesting a veiled sexual attractiveness despite the goddess's dour appearance. Perhaps the clouds hide the true face of the moon, the face of death. The next two lines are an allusion to the myth of Iphigenia, who was a priest-ess of Artemis, the Greek equivalent of Diana, and like Diana also a goddess of the hunt (*33*, p.135). Iphigenia's father, Agamemnon, killed Artemis's favourite stag, the animal sacred to her. As penance he was ordered to sacrifice his daughter, but Artemis snatched Iphigenia from the altar, putting a hind in her place. The "piedra blanca" is the altar, the "ciervo" the substituted hind, and the whole image is a reference to the substitution of one thing for another. The hind of the myth has been turned by Lorca into the masculine stag, which in turn dreams of the possibility of becoming a horse, a symbol of sexual power in Lorca's image system. The figure of the stag, sterile because associated with Diana, thus dreams of potency, a parallel image to the contrast between Diana's hard appearance and her clouded breasts. These lines express a wish for release from sexual frustration, but expressed in a cryptic allusion to classical myth. Yet, while it may be oblique, the use of classical reference in such a calculated manner implies a wish by Lorca to give a universal dimension to his personal experience. Again here we have an example of traditional symbols used in a deliberately enigmatic way to give an appearance of illogicality. The concept behind the image has been transposed into an emotional code.

One of the difficulties of the diction of these poems is its ambiguity. A simple example occurs in the first line of the first poem: "Asesinado por el cielo". Here is another case of paradox: the violent act of assassination has been carried out by a normally un-violent agent. But "cielo" is ambiguous, meaning both sky and heaven. The context of the poem does not only help to decide the ambiguity, and may indeed compound it. Lorca could well have intended to exploit a multivalency of meaning. In this type of poetry one must be ready to accept the simultaneous use of all the meanings and associations of words. Exploitation of ambiguity, multivalency, and the full and free associations of words takes us some way from traditional poetic techniques, and leads us towards the reasons for the oblique, cryptic and distorted character of the New York imagery even when it has links with a traditional poetic mode. The imagery of *Poeta en Nueva York* is perceived with that "heightened perception of disorder and chaos" referred to earlier. It is the product of a distorting, hallucinatory vision.

Let us first examine a single line from "Danza de la muerte": "Enjambres de ventanas acribillaban un muslo de la noche." I suggest that the basic source for this image is an optical illusion, the lit windows of the skyscrapers at night seeming like holes in the darkness. This is now a common phenomenon, but one that in the 1920s, for a European, could perhaps have been experienced only in America, where there were the necessary high-rise buildings. While such an optical effect may explain the genesis of the image it does nothing to explain its significance, which is emotional not conceptual. The windows have been turned into violent, hostile creatures by the animalistic link with swarms. The action of boring holes, produced by association with swarms of stinging insects, is an act of mutilation. The night has been personified by the acquisition of a thigh, and its accompanying erotic associations. The perforated thigh thus becomes an image of sexual mutilation. A simple optical experience has been transformed into an image of violence and conflict because it has been seen with an hallucinatory vision. Here is an instance of distortion that creates emotional intensity. This tiny fragment of American experience has been emotionalised by being passed through the prism of Lorca's anguish. The whole city of New York is seen with the same hallucinated gaze. The exotic un-American fauna Lorca finds in the city is also the product of that same gaze, and of his visits to the Zoo (*1*, I, p.1103). It is not difficult to understand how someone in a state of hypersensitivity would have an immediate emotional reaction to the spectacle of animals from other, healthier, natural environments, trapped in the polluted city. However, nowhere in the poems is there a mention of the Zoo, or even the most oblique allusion to it. Tropical, African animals appear as part of the normal circumstance of the city, as victims of the city's hostility, although they can themselves on occasion present a threat of violence. In his mind Lorca has let the animals out of their cages to become integrated into his experience of the city as a whole. The hallucinated view of the animals can be seen clearly in another image from "Danza de la muerte": "los camellos de carne desgarrada." When a camel moults its fur hangs from its body in long skeins; I suggest Lorca has noted this at the Zoo, but then the image has been emotionalised, the fur transposed into torn flesh, another image of suffering and mutilation.

The most striking example of this hallucinatory vision of New York occurs in the "Paisaje de la multitud que vomita", which has the subtitle "Anochecer de Coney Island". This poem seems to be almost a surrealist "texto onírico", the transcription of a nightmare experience with Lorca alone in the midst of a drunken, vomiting crowd. Yet it is not a dream experience at all but the direct product of a visit to the fairground on Coney Island on a Sunday. Lorca described the fair in a lecture he gave after his return from America:

> Coney Island es una gran feria a la cual los domingos de verano acuden más de un millón de criaturas. Beben, gritan, comen, se revuelcan y dejan el mar lleno de periódicos y las calles abarrotadas de latas, de cigarros apagados, de mordiscos de zapatos sin tacón. Vuelve la muchedumbre de la feria cantando, y vomita en grupos de cien personas apoyadas sobre las barandillas y orina en grupos de mil en los rincones, sobre las barcas abandonadas y sobre el monumento de Garibaldi o del soldado desconocido. (*1*, I, p.1100)

This statement is a calculated exaggeration, an exaggeration that is greatly increased in the poem derived from the experience. The

crowds at the fair have been distorted by the poet's emotionalised
vision, which has turned the revellers into subhuman creatures, fit
inhabitants of the city, who pollute the natural world and are specifically charged with an act of sacrilege against the monuments to the
human spirit of freedom and self-sacrifice. The direct reference to
Garibaldi and the Unknown Soldier introduces political and social
overtones to the condemnation. The distorted vision of the crowd
has an ethical as well as an emotional function.

Coney Island, the animals in the Zoo, the windows of a skyscraper
at night, the whole city of New York, are exploited by Lorca as
devices for expressing his emotional disturbance. The psychological
process outlined above is similar to that of the objective correlative,
which can in fact frequently be seen at work in these poems. Jorge
Guillén has told how one image is owed to a remark made by his
small son Claudio while out walking with Lorca several years before
he went to New York. As they passed the site of some demolished
buildings on the outskirts of Valladolid, the three-year old Claudio
had declared: "Ahí meriendan los borrachos" (*1*, I, pp.LXXIX-
LXXX). This phrase appears twice in *Poeta en Nueva York*: "por el
derribo de los cielos yertos/donde meriendan muerte los borrachos"
("Vaca"), and "por los blancos derribos de Júpiter donde meriendan
muerte los borrachos" ("Fábula y rueda de los tres amigos"). Know-
ing without doubt the source of this image it is possible to see clearly
the process of elaboration that has taken place. The substance of
the drunks' meal has been specified as death, and in the first instance
quoted the demolition site has acquired cosmic, or possibly metaphysical, proportions, depending on how "cielo" is interpreted. The
chance remark of a young child has been enlarged by a process of
emotionalisation to become an image of despair, and possibly of
apostasy. The second example is a completely parallel image, although seemingly with more arbitrary additions than the first. The
apparently strange presence of Jupiter can be explained simply by
his function as god the father in the classical pantheon; he is therefore
the equivalent of "cielos" in the first example. White in the image
could be a simple reminiscence of the demolition site, but white is
also the colour sacred to Jupiter, and therefore certainly not an
arbitrary decoration. The mention of Jupiter would also indicate that
"cielos" in the poem "Vaca" is designed to have a strong religious

reference. The collapse of heaven brings down with it any hope of consolation for death that might have been held out to a degraded humanity. The rationalisation of this image made possible by our knowledge of its source, its duplication in alternative forms, and its use of an objective symbol system of classical reference, is of course nothing more than an explanation. The true significance of the image is its emotional force that comes from the compression, and thus the suppression of the rational element in its process of elaboration.

There are occasions, however, when Lorca can deliberately seek the expression of illogicality, and the chance conjunction of incongruous elements cultivated by surrealism. The technique commonly used on such occasions is a disparity between the syntactic structure and the semantic content of a phrase, as in the following example from "Panorama ciego de Nueva York":

> Si no son los pájaros
> cubiertos de ceniza,
> si no son los gemidos que golpean las ventanas de la boda,
> serán las delicadas criaturas del aire
> que manan la sangre nueva por la oscuridad inextinguible.
> Pero no, no son los pájaros,
> porque los pájaros están a punto de ser bueyes;
> pueden ser rocas blancas con la ayuda de la luna
> y son siempre muchachos heridos
> antes de que los jueces levanten la tela.

The "si no son" structure beginning this passage has the clear ring of Góngora, and as in Góngora it is used as a peg on which to hang imagery, although the images now are very different from those of the seventeenth century. The positive symbol of the birds is negated by association with ash. The groans rattling the windows are a substitution for the birds beating on the windows, an emotionalisation of the birds as an image of sadness and suffering, here set starkly in contrast to the wedding as a symbol of happiness and fertility, from which the window separates them. The "delicadas criaturas del aire" are a positive statement of the image of the birds, what they should be if they were not negated by the preceding distorting images. The image of new blood could have associations of violence, although I prefer to see it as an image of birth, and thus of fertility linked with the wedding. "Oscuridad inextinguible" is a paradox for the everlasting darkness which will presumably overwhelm the fertility symbol of the blood. The birds then turn into oxen, into castrated bulls, a sterility symbol negating again the positive meaning of the birds. With the aid of the moon, the standard Lorcan agent of death, the birds can also become "rocas blancas", perhaps an image for the gravestone, but in any case something that will deny them the faculty of flight. This complex sequence of images ends with a statement of the one permanent element in the situation; all of the preceding images are the equivalent of "muchachos heridos", an image of wounded innocence now transferred unequivocally to a human dimension with, in view of Lorca's homosexuality, associations with the loss of sexual innocence. "Los jueces levanten la tela" seems to be an elaboration of the phrase "poner en tela de juicio" combined with "levantar el telón", bringing together associations of doubt, judgement mixed with menace, and the comedy of life. The effectiveness of this sequence of images is wrought largely by the tension between the syntactic structure normally used in the context of logical discourse and the illogical relationships between the images which defy the causal links of the syntax. The effect is disconcerting, and this perhaps is the ultimate meaning of the image sequence, as an expression of the perturbation in the poet's experience.

A similar tension between form and content occurs in other statements that use concessive clauses. In "Danza de la muerte", for example:

> Porque si la rueda olvida su fórmula,
> ya puede cantar desnuda con las manadas de caballos:
> y si una llama quema los helados proyectos,
> el cielo tendrá que huir ante el tumulto de las ventanas.

Here again the syntax of discursive argument has been filled with elements that bear no rational links, so much so that it is difficult to offer an interpretation of these lines. The second concessive statement is easier to explain in part. The "helados proyectos" could be read as failed dreams, destroyed by an antagonistic force, flame being the opposite of ice. "El tumulto de las ventanas" recalls the swarms of windows discussed earlier, the windows of the skyscrapers activated into hostility. The menacing presence of the city has chased away the sky/heaven as a result of the destruction of dreams. The parallelism of the two concessive clauses should indicate that the first has the same import as the second, though it is difficult to see precisely how. "Manadas de caballos" could parallel the tumult of windows, except that horses tend to have positive associations for Lorca. "La rueda", a highly ambiguous term, singing naked with the horses, could be an image of the loss of sexual inhibition. In which case the first concessive clause has the opposite emotional tenor to the second, making the image sequence as a whole even more complicated than at first sight. But the difficulty of this sequence is such that its significance can only be a matter of conjecture. What is interesting here, however, is the device of the "if" clause containing two rationally unconnected elements. This was a technique employed by French surrealists, and the substance of one of their games, which was a form of literary "Consequences". A piece of paper was folded down the middle and different people wrote on the two halves the separate parts of concessive or causal clauses, so producing strange juxtapositions. We have thus seen the imagery and diction of *Poeta en Nueva York* move through a very wide range of techniques, from the directly traditional to those actually employed by orthodox surrealists.

II Innocence lost and kept

The first section of *Poeta en Nueva York* has a completely personal
focus and not a single specifically American reference, apart from
the apt title "Poemas de la soledad en Columbia University". All is a
contemplation of the self, and of the poet's childhood self in particular. The section's rubric gives some clue to its character. The lines
"Furia color de amor, /amor color de olvido", by Luis Cernuda, are
the evocation of a disastrous failure of love, and may thus be taken
as an indicator of the "penumbra sentimental" from which Lorca
was suffering at the time. All the poems in this section express a
painful disillusionment.

In a deliberately structured book the opening poem can be
expected to have a special significance; "Vuelta de paseo" could be
taken as a basic theme statement. We have already noted the bitterly
ironic awareness of violent deception in the paradox and ambiguity
of the first line. I read line 4, "dejaré crecer mis cabellos", as a
metaphor for death: the hair of the corpse continuing to grow after
the assassination. The syntactic parallel of lines 2 and 3, "entre las
formas que van hacia la sierpe / y las formas que buscan el cristal",
contains an apparent semantic contrast between "sierpe" and
"cristal". This may be illuminated by a repeated use of the images
in another poem, "Nocturno del hueco": "y eran duro cristal
definitivo / las formas que buscan el giro de la sierpe." "Definitivo"
is an adjective associated elsewhere with death ("Paisaje de la multitude que orina"), and "cristal" too may thus be taken as a death
image. In Lorca's usage the snake almost always has malevolent
associations, linked with the Christian symbol of evil. If both
"sierpe" and "cristal" are negative then the poet is faced with a
choice of two evils. In a later poem, "Danza de la muerte", there is
a reference to two death-forces, the "ímpetu primitivo" and the
"ímpetu mecánico", the death that is a force of nature and the new
death-force found in the dehumanised world of New York. I suggest
that "sierpe" and "cristal" are alternative formulations of the old and
the new forces of death.

The images that follow in three parallel couplets are specific elabor-
ations of the vague and abstract "formas" of the opening lines.
"Con el árbol de muñones que no canta / y el niño con el blanco
rostro de huevo" presents images of mutilation in both a natural and
a human dimension. The pollarded tree is songless because the birds
have been amputated along with the branches. The child with a
white, egg-like, featureless face is reminiscent of the mannequins in
the paintings of Giorgio di Chirico; certainly this image could be
taken as a self-sufficient entity, the personage of a surrealist dream-
world. It could also be an image of a lack of identity, or, through
the link with the pollarded tree, of a loss of identity, an area of
meaning augmented by the association of the egg with fragility. The
child with the vulnerable, featureless face could represent Lorca's
own lost childhood.

Parallel images of mutilation occur in the next couplet: "Con los
animalitos de cabeza rota / y el agua harapienta de los pies secos."
The animals with broken heads evoke associations with the child's
egg-like face, while the personified water, commented on earlier,
combines both the human and the natural reference. This fusion is
summarised in the third couplet: "Con todo lo que tiene cansancio
sordomudo / y mariposa ahogada en el tintero." "Cansancio sordomudo" is an image of sense deprivation for which we are already
prepared by the child's featureless face. The butterfly drowned in
an inkwell is another image of violence done to a creature of the
natural world, but it has additional associations. A butterfly is a
common symbolist image of the ideal, used as such in Lorca's first
play *El maleficio de la mariposa*. It has been suggested that the inkwell could symbolise literary activity and the drowned butterfly thus
represent the impotence of poetry (*24*, p.11). The songlessness of
the trees earlier could have similar associations. Certainly the close
of the poem sharpens the personal focus: "Tropezando con mi rostro
distinto de cada día. / ¡Asesinado por el cielo!" Here is an expression of disorientation, narcissism and alienation, as the contemplated
face changes daily with an ironic echo of the Lord's Prayer. We have
here a possible allusion to a crisis of identity that may be compared
to the sentiments in the letter written by Lorca on his way to
America, quoted in the previous chapter. The exclamatory repetition
of the poem's opening line gives to its paradox a note of pained

surprise and injustice. "Vuelta de paseo" is a concise statement of
the violence and mutilation, the alienation and the sense of deception,
the feeling of lost innocence, and the threat of death, all elaborated
in the course of *Poeta en Nueva York*.

The second poem focusses directly on Lorca's lost childhood. The
title "1910" refers to the year when he would have been twelve years
old, while the subtitle "Intermedio" points ironically at the transitori-
ness of childhood. The poem's opening statement clearly asserts the
child's innocence of death: "Aquellos ojos míos de mil novecientos
diez / no vieron enterrar a los muertos." The second stanza lists a
series of death symbols from the poet's Spanish background: a
poisonous mushroom, the moon, the dried slices of lemon in a bar.
Then in stanza 3 the concern changes to the child's innocence of
sexuality, with the introduction of the erotic symbol of the horse,
and of Santa Rosa de Lima, who is also given an erotic dimension
by association with the other images. It has been suggested that the
last line of this stanza refers to Lorca being told as a child that the
noise of cats copulating in the garden of his house was the result of
the cats having eaten frogs (*24*, p.17). If this is so, an allusion to an
anecdote of childhood has been made an image of adult sexual guilt.

The fourth stanza makes the point that the child's innocence of
death and sexuality have long since disappeared, discarded with other
useless things in the attic of his past, which is described in an image
of disillusion as "el sitio donde el sueño tropezaba con su realidad".
The sense of deception is repeated in the final stanza: "He visto que
las cosas / cuando buscan su curso encuentran su vacío." The poem
ends on a note of unrestrained lament for the disappearance of the
past and its legacy of present solitude. The memories of the past
are now empty bodies, clothes that contain no flesh, no naked
innocence: "Hay un dolor de huecos por el aire sin gente / y en mis
ojos criaturas vestidas ¡sin desnudo!"

The past is also evoked in the third poem of the book, and one so
difficult that its significance is something of a matter for conjecture.
The title, "Rueda y fábula de los tres amigos", alludes to a children's
ring game, an allusion supported by techniques of parallelism and
repetition in the poem's structure. But as a whole it seems to refer
to the days of youth rather than childhood. Something clearly
unpleasant has happened to the three friends; they are described

successively as "helados . . . quemados . . . enterrados . . . momifica-
dos", in which can be seen a certain progression from pain into death.
They seem to be associated with three separate areas of experience.
The images connected with Lorenzo point to the social world: "el
mundo de las universidades sin tejados . . . las bolas de billar."
Emilio is associated with pain, "las heridas de las manos . . . el mundo
de la sangre y los alfileres blancos", and Enrique with death, "el
mundo de los muertos . . . los ojos vacíos de los pájaros". The three
friends are made to disappear from the poem by the children's song
technique of counting down from three to none. The frame of
reference then becomes emphatically personal. It has been suggested
that the bullfighting imagery in the lines "Yo había matado la quinta
luna / y bebían agua por las fuentes los abanicos y los aplausos"
alludes to the immense popular success of the *Romancero gitano*
(*24*, p.33). It is possible to calculate that the *Romancero gitano* was
Lorca's fifth volume of verse. This seems an attractive interpretation.
There follows the imagery of sexual repression in the reference to
Diana and the myth of Iphigenia commented on earlier.

   In the poem's final stanza it is the poet himself who has died. The
closing lines contain a reference to the Day of Judgement, when the
sea shall give up its dead, and a possible reference to *Poeta en Nueva
York* itself, if the sixth moon is Lorca's sixth book of poems. Certainly the concepts of flight and violence here encapsulate the emotional nature of the New York poems and their departure from the
previous style. "Fábula y rueda de los tres amigos" ends on a directly
personal note, and this, paradoxically, may explain the strangely
impersonal beginning. I suggest that this poem is in part a reflection
of the crisis of identity that lies behind the book as a whole, a crisis
which involved the success of the *Romancero gitano*. If such is the
case then the three friends can be read as projections of Lorca's own
youth, partial or alternative selves now lost, images of lost identity.

   "Tu infancia en Mentón" is another very cryptic poem. The
rubric, "Sí, tu niñez ya fábula de fuentes", is a celebration of childhood taken from a well-known poem by Jorge Guillén. Lorca's use
of this line as a refrain has a heavy, almost sarcastic, irony, for his
poem is far removed from the ingenuous wonder of a child. Lines
9-10, for example, evoke erotic disillusionment and frustration,

given a specifically homosexual point by the reference to Apollo: "Norma de amor te di, hombre de Apolo, / llanto con ruiseñor enajenado."

The failure of the sexual dream is repeated more emphatically in lines 32-7:

No me tapen la boca los que buscan
espigas de Saturno por la nieve
o castran animales por un cielo,
clínica y selva de la anatomía.

The castrated animals are a clear image of sexual inhibition, ironically associated here with the ambiguous sky/heaven already seen in "Vuelta de paseo". Saturn was the god of seed-time and harvest, while the ear of corn is a traditional symbol of fertility. But the ear of corn will not be found in the cold snow, an image of sterility in the New York poems. The feeling of inhibition is sharply summarised in the despairing negation: "¡Amor de siempre, amor, amor de nunca!"

The four "poems of solitude" which begin *Poeta en Nueva York* are concerned with pain, suffering, lost childhood and the loss of sexual innocence. They are intensely personal poems, with a focus on the self that is an indication of solitude. The self-centred concern also points to the problem of identity which appears explicitly on several occasions. These opening poems examine the poet's state of mind produced by experience prior to the journey to America and establish the disillusionment already affecting him when he arrived there. A preoccupation with innocence, both lost and kept, is also a marked feature of poems dealing directly with the American experience.

"Poema doble del lago Edem", from section IV of the book, carries a rubric from Garcilaso, as might befit a poem written during Lorca's stay in Vermont. Although he mis-spells Eden Mills the significance of the place name was not lost on him. This is not a double poem but a poem that splits the poet's personality into two, his past and present. He laments, in the second stanza, the loss of a former voice, a voice of innocence, childhood and truth. The lament also contains clear references to Adam in Paradise before the Fall; allusions are made to Eve's creation from Adam's rib and to Adam's naming of the plants, and to a time before the existence of the Lorcan sexual symbol of the horse. Two stanzas later there is a plea to be allowed to return to the Garden of Eden, freed from the sexual guilt that brought about Man's eviction. But the Eden now sought has distinct pagan characteristics, symbolised by Panic fauns and the sexual freedom they represent:

Déjame pasar, hombrecillo de los cuernos,
al bosque de los desperezos
y los alegrísimos saltos.

The poem's ninth stanza establishes a link between poetry and the poet's identity:

Quiero llorar diciendo mi nombre,
rosa, niño y abeto a la orilla de este lago,
para decir mi verdad de hombre de sangre
matando en mí la burla y la sugestión del vocablo.

The former existence in the past is regarded as representing the true self which has been lost or betrayed. The reference to "la burla y la sugestión del vocablo" I take as a criticism of the obliqueness of the diction both in *Poeta en Nueva York* and in much of the earlier poetry. The stanza quoted above is preceded by the exclamation: "¡Oh voz antigua, quema con tu lengua/esta voz de hojalata y de talco!" The strange reference to talc is explained by the presence of a talc mine near Eden Mills (*9*, p.131). The anguished concern with lost childhood and lost innocence is again directly involved with a problem of identity.

In view of Lorca's preoccupation with his loss of innocence it is not surprising to find the same concern in his attitude towards the inhabitants of America. Most of them have fallen from grace, but two categories of people do maintain their innocence, the Blacks and children. In his 1932 lecture Lorca described the Blacks of Harlem as the one section of New York society which upholds the values of religion, faith and spirituality:

Pese a quien pese [los negros] son lo más espiritual y delicado de aquel mundo. Porque creen, porque esperan, porque cantan y porque tienen una exquisita pureza religiosa que los salva de todos sus peligrosos afanes actuales . . . Lo que yo miraba, paseaba, y soñaba era el gran barrio negro de Harlem . . . donde lo lúbrico tiene un acento de inocencia que lo hace perturbador y religioso. (*1*, I, pp.1096-7)

Two poems of the section "Los negros" are concerned entirely with this Black world. "Norma y paraíso de los negros" is in part an evocation of race consciousness created by a contrast between the verbs "odian" and "aman", and by contrasting colour images. In stanza 1 images of whiteness, the cheek and the "salón de la nieve

fría" (ice-cream parlour?), are set against images of nature which are
in conflict or are diminished, like the bird reduced to a shadow. The
Blacks' love, as described in stanza 4, is centred on nature with which
they have a particularly close relationship:

> Con la ciencia del tronco y del rastro
> llenan de nervios luminosos la arcilla
> y patinan lúbricos por agua y arenas
> gustando la amarga frescura de su milenaria savia.

The skating here may perhaps allude to roller skating, or ice skating,
in Central Park, novelties for a Spaniard. The adjective "lúbricos"
should be read in the light of its use in the 1932 lecture quoted above,
where pejorative associations are annulled by the Blacks' innocence.
They have maintained contact with the primal life-force in the
natural world, a contact which the Whites have, by implication, lost.

Just as white is the dominant colour motif in the first two stanzas,
which begin with the verb "odian", the statements in the following
stanzas, which depend on the verb "aman", turn to the colour blue
used as an image of paradise. Thus in stanza 5 blue is an image of
timelessness where the white of day does not disturb the preferred
blackness of night. The wind that was in conflict in the opening
stanza is now naked, freed of sexual guilt, sweeping away the clouds,
transposed into camels from the Zoo and made empty to represent
failure and disillusionment. Timelessness and sexual innocence
point to a recovery of Man's state before the Fall. Paradise is
presented in the basically symbolist image of the clear blue sky, but
this may also have specifically American connotations. We could
have here a reference to the Blues, an apt allusion to Black culture.
It is know that Lorca used to visit a Harlem nightclub called, significantly, "Small's Paradise" (2, p.34). There is, however, a strange
ambivalence to be found in many of the images of this poem:

> Aman el azul desierto,
> las vacilantes expresiones bovinas,
> la mentirosa luna de los polos . . .

The empty sky can be given both a positive and a negative significance, the adjective "bovinas" is associated, as we shall see later, with
sacrificial victims, while the moon brings an inevitable tone of
menace, although this may be softened by "mentirosa". There is a
sense of restriction weighing on the Black paradise.

Ambivalence and restriction are marked features of the "Oda al rey de Harlem". The opening lines present a considerable puzzle:

Con una cuchara,
arrancaba los ojos a los cocodrilos
y golpeaba el trasero de los monos.
Con una cuchara.

This is an incantatory, almost magical, statement centred on the African animals of the Zoo. Crocodiles are associated with death in the New York poems, and their blinding may thus be taken to represent a defeat for death. Monkeys are a traditional symbol of trouble, while in Christian symbology they stand for sin, lasciviousness, malice, the base condition of man, and even for the Devil. Their chastisement seems to indicate another defeat for negative forces. The spoon is perhaps an image of the King's sceptre, diminished in status.

The next three stanzas contain a sequence of images of the corruption or destruction of nature; beetles are drunk on anisette, water is polluted, roses flee. Worst of all: "los niños machacaban pequeñas ardillas / con un rubor de frenesí manchado." The defenceless creatures of nature are destroyed by the children who should be their innocent human counterparts; "manchado" is a transferred epithet from "rubor". But such mayhem takes place only in the world of the Whites.

The fifth and sixth stanzas are instructions to escape from White society, by crossing the bridges from the Bronx into Harlem on Manhattan Island. There can be found "el rubor negro" in direct contrast to the tainted "rubor" of the Whites. There can be found the still uncorrupted life-force of nature, the "caliente piña". Lorca calls for the death of the agents of corruption, the "rubio vendedor de aguardiente", who may well be responsible for the beetles' drunkenness, and the "amigos de la manzana y de la arena", where the sand is an image of fear and the apple an image of sexual guilt. The destruction of these hostile figures will enable the King of Harlem to proclaim his position, by singing with the crowd of his subjects, and so stilling the active presence of death in the city as the crocodiles are made to sleep beneath a moon associated with asbestos, the poisonous material of an industrial society. This dreamed victory over death will release from their bondage the

Blacks enslaved in the service of White society as menial kitchen servants. This dream is, however, cut short by the lament in stanza 7 for the repression of the Blacks, in which the image of darkness as repressed light, and the images of sense deprivation, culminate in the paradox of the King in a janitor's uniform. But the King is himself an image of power, power prefigured in the reference to blood and violence, and the repression of such power implies an enormous potential for destruction should the bonds containing it be broken.

The ode's second section commences with another denunciation of White society. The American night is split, an image of the mutilation of nature. American girls are pregnant with money as well as with children, corrupting their fertility with materialism. The whisky the Whites drink is linked with the Lorcan death symbol of silver, while the ice in the glass becomes pieces of the human heart, transubstantiated by the poet's emotional and ethical denunciation.

In the five remaining stanzas of this section the idea of violent destruction, implied earlier, is invoked in an emphatic litany of images of death. The blood becomes here an all-pervading agent of death emanating from the natural world, "el tuétano del bosque", and bringing nature's revenge on the society that has ignored or corrupted the values of nature.

The ode's final section focusses on the moment of the city's apocalyptic destruction. As an impassable wall grows all round the city the poet advises the Blacks not to seek to escape but to search for their salvation within the natural world:

> Buscad el gran sol del centro
> hechos una piña zumbadora.
> El sol que se desliza por los bosques
> seguro de no encontrar una ninfa,
> el sol que destruye números y no ha cruzado nunca un sueño,
> el tatuado sol que baja por el río
> y muge seguido de caimanes.

Here we have a return of the image of the pineapple, linked now through the adjective "zumbadora" with the life symbol of the bee. The sun, free from negative influences (represented by nymphs in these American poems), and hostile to materialism, is the life-force of nature, a tattooed, primal, precivilised force. This powerful life-force has tamed the caymans, the American crocodile and an image of death. The advice to the Blacks is clear: turn away from the false values of the city and seek a communion with the elemental world of nature.

The closing stanzas examine what will happen when the Blacks inherit the world after the city's destruction. They are advised not to fear death, since it is an entirely natural phenomenon: "Jamás sierpe, ni cebra, ni mula/palidecieron al morir." When the city has been razed the Blacks will be able to take possession of the technological society from which they had been excluded, and reabsorb it into nature:

> Entonces, negros, entonces, entonces,
> podréis besar con frenesí las ruedas de las bicicletas,
> poner parejas de microscopios en las cuevas de las ardillas
> y danzar al fin, sin duda, mientras las flores erizadas
> asesinan a nuestro Moisés casi en los juncos del cielo.

Note that Moses, the archpriest of White society, is killed by normally tranquil flowers, agents of nature, made angry and aggressive by the adjective "erizadas". The death of Moses before entering the Promised Land is made contemporaneous with the incident of his infancy in the bullrushes, giving a great complexity of association to "cielo". The ambiguous sky/heaven becomes in addition the Promised Land and the lost paradise of infancy, and all of these meanings are made void by the link with Moses. There will be no entry into the White Kingdom of Heaven, and the Blacks dance in celebration of this.

The poem ends with a return of the tone of lament, yet what remains most in the mind is the threat of apocalyptic violence. Lorca here is taking on a prophetic voice, but his vision sees the poor and the oppressed taking over the world of their masters after it has been destroyed by the violence bred by poverty and oppression. This is not residence in the Heavenly Kingdom as recompense for earthly suffering, but the taking of an earthly kingdom by force, a quasi-Marxist rather than a Christian view of things. There is undoubtedly a social focus in this poem, but the real condemnation of the Whites' treatment of the Harlem Blacks is made on ethical grounds. The Blacks are still in touch with the values in which Lorca himself believes and which he sees having been forsaken or corrupted by the White society of New York.

The American Black then, despite his situation of servitude, is not part of the corrupt world of the city. Another surviving innocent is the child, like the young boy who gave his name to the poem "El niño Stanton", one of the Vermont poems included in section V, "En la cabaña del farmer". Lorca expresses his sense of identification with the ten-year-old boy, who is an innocent surrounded by a host of death images. The most notable agent of death is cancer, an image peculiar to the New York poems: "el vivísimo cáncer lleno de nubes y termómetros / con su casto afán de manzana para que lo piquen los ruiseñores." Here the apple, that Christian symbol of sexual guilt, is specifically associated with chastity, and would, presumably, be injurious to the bird of love, the nightingale. The child is, however, safe from the malevolence around him, protected by his innocence and his association with the innocents of nature: "¡Oh mi Stanton, idiota y bello entre los pequeños animalitos!" The child is advised, like the Blacks, to detach himself from corrupt White society and to seek redemption in the values of nature, where he will find the heavenly words forgotten by his own people. Lorca, nonetheless, sees no hope for his own salvation. He sees himself in the process of dying:

> Mi agonía buscaba su traje,
> polvorienta, mordida por los perros,
> y tú la acompañaste sin temblar
> hasta la puerta del agua oscura.

The image of the lost suit, torn and dusty, introduces again the theme of the identity crisis, linked yet once more with the loss of childhood, as the young American boy with whom the poet identifies becomes the representative of a former innocent self. While Stanton will survive if he heeds the poet's advice, the poet himself will not escape death.

III Corte y aldea: *death and disbelief*

The setting of *Poeta en Nueva York* alternates between the city itself and the countryside in Vermont. In both situations Lorca finds
a dominance of death, seen frequently against an absence or failure
of religious faith. "Calles y sueños", the book's third section, is a
criticism of the city's polluted spiritual environment.

New York is seen as the city of things dead and of an active force
of death. In "Danza de la muerte" what is perhaps a reminiscence of
a carnival procession is turned into a fusion of the medieval Dance of
Death and an African tribal ritual. The dance is dominated by an
African mask, which is, in the poet's own words:

> El mascarón típico africano, muerte verdaderamente muerte, sin
> ángeles ni *resurrexit*. Muerte alejada de todo espíritu, bárbara y
> primitiva como los Estados Unidos, que no han luchado ni lucha-
> rán por el cielo. (*1*, I, p.1099)

The poem's opening section lists a series of nature images which have
been negated by the presence of death. Dead animals join the dance,
African animals from the Zoo. A hippopotamus is negated by its
"pezuñas de ceniza", a symbolic transposition of the animal's muddy
feet, while a gazelle has the death-image of an everlasting flower in
its throat. When the dance reaches Wall Street, in the poem's
second section, it encounters the city's inhuman materialism, a
world of "obreros parados" and "borrachos de plata". The confront-
ation of America's financial capital with the African death-mask
presents no incongruity for Lorca:

> No es extraño para la danza
> este columbario que pone los ojos amarillos.
> De la esfinge a la caja de caudales hay un hilo tenso
> que atraviesa el corazón de todos los niños pobres.

These lines deliberately link the ancient world, in the images of the
Roman funerary niche and the Greek Sphynx, with the new world
of the Stock Exchange, both of which bring suffering to the weak
and the poor. The world of machine society joins the dance with the
mask, the death of the human spirit embraces the forces of primal,
physical death: "El ímpetu primitivo baila con el ímpetu mecánico, /

ignorantes en su frenesí de la luz original." "Luz original" could
have a religious significance, a possibility strengthened by other
allusions; the "cielo vacío . . . mondado y puro, idéntico a sí mismo"
at the beginning of the poem's second section, and the reference to
the Nativity in stanza 2 of the final section. The Christmas story (the
poem is dated "diciembre 1929") is heavy with images of foreboding.
The drop of blood foreshadows the Crucifixion, the "muerte semilla
de manzana" alludes to the Fall and consequent subjection to
Death; in Christian tradition Adam is frequently regarded as a pre-
figuration of Christ. The mollusc without a shell is a striking image
of vulnerability.

Immediately after this strong religious allusion comes an emphatic statement that the dancers are not the normal dead but the living
dead of the city. The poet then instructs that neither the traditional
members of the Dance of Death, the Pope and the King, nor more
modern members, like the millionaire, should take part. Only the
African mask should remain. The poem culminates in a prophecy of
the city's violent destruction as it is invaded by cobras and lianas,
avenging elements of the jungle.

Ethical criticism of the city through religious allusion is made
very direct in "La aurora". The traditional symbol of hope in the
dawn is associated with negated positive symbols, "negras palomas"
and "aguas podridas", and is itself personified as a creature of pain,
moaning as it descends the fire-escapes, a striking emotionalisation
of the visual image of the shadow moving down a building as the sun
rises. The dawn, moreover, seeks an image of Andalusian innocence,
the white flower of the spikenard. The dawn is then directly equated
with the Host of the Mass: "La aurora llega y nadie la recibe en su
boca / porque allí no hay mañana ni esperanza posible." This dawn
is clearly an image for the Light of the World, although in New York
there would seem to be no possibility of the redemption from death
that His Coming should signify. The awareness of death, described
as the knowledge in one's bones, means there will be no paradise,
nor "amores deshojados", an allusion to freedom from sexual guilt
in a return to Eden. All that remains in the city is the destruction of
hope by a material, industrial society that has no roots in the natural
world.

The impotence of religious consolation is expressed with great emphasis in "Ciudad sin sueño":

No duerme nadie por el cielo. Nadie, nadie.
No duerme nadie.
Las criaturas de la luna huelen y rondan sus cabañas.
Vendrán las iguanas vivas a morder a los hombres que no sueñan
y el que huye con el corazón roto encontrará por las esquinas
al increíble cocodrilo quieto bajo la tierna protesta de los astros.

Nietzsche's declaration that God is dead has frequently provoked the
joking response that if He is not dead then He must be asleep. Lorca
is declaring that since there is no God in Heaven then man is the
helpless prey of death whose agents are more animals from the Zoo.
The poem plays with the ambiguity of "sueño", meaning both sleep
and dream; dreams are positive for Lorca but a lack of sleep always
has negative connotations for him. The literary allusion "No es
sueño la vida", which begins the third stanza, has thus a strong element of irony in its contradiction of the title of Calderón's play.
The religious sentiment here is strengthened by the biblical tone of
the stanza's last two lines: "y al que le duele su dolor le dolerá sin
descanso / y al que teme la muerte la llevará sobre sus hombros."
    The next two stanzas seem to deal with the Second Coming and
the Day of Judgement but no genuine resurrection is produced and
the poem turns back in on itself. The dead are taken back into
death: "hay que llevarlos al muro donde iguanas y sierpes esperan."
The reason for this is the absence of God and the emptiness of
Heaven, emphatically repeated in the final stanza. I find in the
closing lines an oblique reference to the Church and to negated
images of the Mass. Chalices are "copas falsas" that hold poison not
blood and the Host is not the flesh of Christ but a skull representing
death triumphant. The theatrical references imply the deceit of the
Church in offering false hopes of salvation.
    The concern in "Calles y sueños" with things spiritual rather than
things temporal is confirmed in "Panorama ciego de Nueva York".
The opening stanza has already received comment in the first chapter
of this study. The second stanza makes a most interesting statement
differentiating the pain provoked by the awareness of death from an
even deeper metaphysical disturbance, associated with images of
insomnia and eye mutilation:

El verdadero dolor que mantiene despiertas las cosas
es una pequeña quemadura infinita

en los ojos inocentes de los otros sistemas.

The following stanza is composed of a sequence of images stressing the absurdity of life. People are empty bodies, discarded suits of clothes herded together by the sky/heaven. Women who die in childbirth are made aware that all life is subject to death and suffering. Intellectual inquiry, the philosopher, is also helpless in this situation. Love has virtually disappeared from the world, known only to crippled swallows and innocent, idiot children.

The poem then returns to the image of the birds and the false discursive logic of its beginning. A series of death-images precedes a direct statement of the poet's failure to find "la quemadura que mantiene despiertas las cosas", which I interpret as the answer to the enigma of life. The poet has only found more evidence of death, because the answer was elsewhere:

Pero el verdadero dolor estaba en otras plazas
donde los peces cristalizados agonizaban dentro de los troncos;
plazas del cielo extraño para las antiguas estatuas ilesas . . .

I assume "plaza" to be a bullring because of the association with death. "Plazas del cielo" would thus become a bitterly ironic image. The fish dying in the tree-trunks are, I suggest, an image of fossils seen in a museum. This might also be the provenance of the statues, which I suggest are those of the ancient gods. The total significance of these images comes from their relationship to each other. The crystalised fish represent the destruction of nature but the statues which are unharmed and alien in the "plazas del cielo" present a set of values apart from the Christian context implied by the sky/heaven. This set of images should be seen in the context of the poem's closing lines, where, in an oblique allusion to the Lord's Prayer, the will of the Earth is implicitly contrasted with the will of Heaven, and only that of the Earth declared to exist. Without the metaphysical anguish created by an empty heaven there would be not pain, but the possibility of a terrestrial paradise with ever-open doors leading to a world of abundance and innocence, that image of "rubor" we have seen in other poems. The old gods would be happy in such a situation. Compare the pre-Christian paradise evoked in "Poema doble del lago Edem" and the "amores deshojados" of "La aurora". "Panorama ciego de Nueva York" seems to conclude that there is hope for man if he seeks solace in the life-force of nature, like the young boy Stanton.

Nonetheless some of the poems specifically linked with the New England countryside are among the bleakest in the book. The sixth section is entitled "Introducción a la muerte" and has the subtitle "Poemas de la soledad en Vermont", echoing the title of the book's opening section and identifying the experience of the countryside with the experience of the city. The first poem is simply entitled "Muerte" and deals with life's incapacity to escape from death. The structure of parallel sequences of images presents the concept of struggle which begins the poem. The initial sequence list the efforts of one animal to turn into another, but it is a circular sequence: "caballo - perro - golondrina - abeja - caballo". The horse ends up a horse, that central Lorcan life-symbol, here attempting to evade its own reality. The next sequence takes the positive images, horse, rose, sugar, and links them with images of pain and violence: "Y el caballo, / ¡qué flecha aguda exprime de la rosa!, / ¡qué rosa gris levanta de su belfo!" The sequence horse - rose - sugar leads to a reference to knives as the agents of death seeking to destroy inno-cence: "y los puñales diminutos, / ¡qué luna sin establos, qué des-nudos, / piel eterna y rubor, andan buscando!" We have seen "rubor" used frequently as an image of innocence; "desnudos" has a similar significance, and "piel eterna" should fall into the same category. The completely parallel structure of the poem is then broken in the last three lines:

> Pero el arco de yeso,
> ¡qué grande, qué invisible, qué diminuto!,
> sin esfuerzo.

The "arco de yeso" refers to the plastered-up niche of a Spanish cemetery. It is the awareness of death that breaks the parallel sequence. The attribution to it of contradictory adjectives shows its omnipresence. The final phrase, "sin esfuerzo", mocks the initial quintuple repetition of " ¡qué esfuerzo!". Life struggles desperately to avoid death, but death's domination of life is effortless.

"Nocturno del hueco" provides a more specific diagnosis of Lorca's solitude. At least on one level the poem is a lament for lost love, a sentiment summarised in the opening stanza used in variant forms as a refrain:

> *Para ver que todo se ha ido,*

para ver los huecos y los vestidos,
¡dame tu guante de luna,
tu otro guante perdido en la hierba,
amor mío!

The juxtaposition of "huecos" and "vestidos" evokes the idea of the empty body. The glove brings associations of a love token, negated by the link with the moon. Grass is an image closely connected with death; see the poem "Omega", also written in New York (*1*, I, p.783). The poem then continues with a string of images of death affecting both nature and man, reducing all to suffering, like the pulsating breathing of a frog which is compared to the tremolo of a mandolin. This is followed in the fourth stanza by an image of ritual sacrifice, "En la gran plaza desierta / mugía la bovina cabeza recién cortada", and the image of the glass and the snake used earlier in "Vuelta de paseo".

Stanza 6 shows an increased emotionalism in the sequence of exclamations which ends: " ¡qué cielo sin salida, amor, qué cielo!" This outburst against the ambivalent sky/heaven then gives way to a calmer contemplation of death focussing on the loss of innocence ("manzanas mordidas"). However, the image of innocence as a child's first lament, the cry of birth, is bitterly ironic. The second part of the poem becomes emphatically personal, while the imagery develops the earlier allusion to the bullring. The sexual symbol of the horse is negated: "Con el hueco blanquísimo de un caballo, / crines de ceniza." Other nature images are similarly rendered impotent: "Piel seca de uva neutra y amianto de madrugada." By the end of the poem the poet has become fused with the symbol of the horse in an image of permanent stasis: "Ecuestre por mi vida definitivamente anclada." The concluding lines contain an assertion of the triumph of death: "*No hay siglo nuevo ni luz reciente.*" This evokes an immediate allusion to an absence of religious faith, which strengthens the possibility that line 8 of the poem, "*Canta el gallo y su canto dura más que sus alas*", is a reference to St Peter's denial of Christ (*18*, p.42). The obsessive repetition of the image "hueco" and its associations with the empty body brings to mind the identity crisis linked in other poems with the failure of love. But here the death of love is broadened out to encompass the death of everything in a statement of unremitting pessimism.

The failure of love, an oppressive consciousness of death and an underlying religious concern are also the substance of the poem aptly entitled "Ruina". It begins with a sequence of death images, "luna . . . calavera de caballo . . . manzana oscura . . . arena . . . hierbas". In the fourth stanza a lamb is sacrificed to the grass, and in the next stanza "la primer [*sic*] paloma" is reduced to "la cáscara de pluma y celuloide"; both these images could be allusions to Christ. Then clouds, animalised by the phrase "en manada", are stopped in their tracks by the grief of nature, while the menacing grass begins to invade the sky/heaven. It is presumably the "hijo" of stanza 7 who is transformed into the "amor" of the next stanza and there linked with an image of violence, broken glass and shed blood. The poet and his love are all that remains after the general destruction, but they too will not last long. In the last two stanzas love is asked to prepare its skeleton and to seek its "perfil sin sueño", the stasis of death. This ironically brings some stability to the crisis of identity alluded to in the poem's opening lines: "sin encontrarse, / viajero por su propio torso blanco."

The failure of the erotic dream would also seem to be present in the rather enigmatic poem "Niña ahogada en el pozo", contained in section V, "En la cabaña del farmer". Lorca's explanation that this poem was a response to the drowning of a little girl while he was staying on the farm in Vermont has been categorically denied by Angel del Río (*29*, pp.42-4). However, the image of "el agua que no desemboca", used as an obsessive refrain, does have a factual basis: near the farm was an underground water system which could be heard but not seen (*7*, p.12). Water is a basic sexual/life-symbol for Lorca, as it is for many writers, but here the water is negated, unable to run free, and thus for Lorca an image of inhibition. The idea of the well provides a sequence of circular images throughout the poem, images of enclosure. The opening lines contrast physical death with the image of stagnant water: "Las estatuas sufren por los ojos con la oscuridad de los ataúdes, / pero sufren mucho más por el agua que no desemboca." The statues, deactivated human forms, suffer a visual disturbance, an allusion to blindness, due to the consciousness of death. But what is more disturbing is the repression of the sexual life-force. This is the import of the poem, a symbolic drowning in the stilled waters, a point which becomes clearer towards the end of

the poem: "Pero el pozo te alarga manecitas de musgo, / insospe-
chada ondina de casta ignorancia." The girl's inactivity is in contrast
to the activation of the well in the death-image of the moss (compare
the use of "musgo" in "Danza de la muerte", "Ciudad sin sueño"
and "El niño Stanton"). The girl has been transformed into a water-
nymph, and nymphs are negative creatures in the New York poems
(compare "Oda al rey de Harlem", "Paisaje con dos tumbas y un
perro asirio" and "Grito hacia Roma"). The water-nymph has the
quality of chaste innocence, something negative for Lorca. The
poem ends with images of failure and desolation: stagnant water,
stringless violins, pain and emptiness.

Returning to "Introducción a la muerte":   the relationship
of love and death is also the subject of "Luna y panorama de los
insectos", which has the bitterly ironic subtitle "Poema de amor".
The initial series of false concessive clauses in which the two parts of
the statement have no causal link creates an atmosphere of disorientation. This culminates in the line from stanza 3, "Noche igual de la
nieve, de los sistemas suspendidos", where the uneasy juxtaposition
of the darkness of night with the cold, white sterility of snow is
followed by an image of stasis. The tone and style then change
abruptly with the emphatic appearance of the death symbol of the
moon:

Y la luna.
¡La luna!
Pero no la luna.
La raposa de las tabernas,
el gallo japonés que se comió los ojos,
las hierbas masticadas.

The false negative in the third line quoted above leads into an enumeration reminiscent of children's nonsense rhymes, although the
cockerel which consumes its own eyes, and the final image of grass,
sharpen the emotional tone and reassert the presence of death.

The fourth stanza declares a lack of faith in mystic or metaphysical solutions. Only life and death really exist. I read "las
solitarias en los vidrios" as a complex image of saints in stained-
glass windows and crystal-ball gazers. The metaphysician's enquiry
in a herbalist's shop for an alternative form of heaven adds a wry
note of irony, and also brings an echo of the death-image "hierbas".

The stanza then continues with a sequence of death-images that ends in a reference to love as a promethean vulture. The next stanza, in italics, picks up the emotionalised personal reference with an almost hysterical appearance of the crisis of identity: "*Rostro. ¡Tu rostro! Rostro.*" The natural world is reduced to miniscule proportions while that face expands to cover the heavens. The third-person verbs which begin the stanza, and end it with exclamatory violence, produce a sense of menacing activity from external, hostile forces.

The import of stanza 6 is largely a matter for conjecture, although it does seem to urge the need to escape and one notices again the sacrificial image of the wounded cow here linked with the biblical ram's horn. However, the force of the next stanza is strikingly clear:

En mi pañuelo he sentido el tris
de la primera vena que se rompe.
Cuida tus pies, amor mío, ¡tus manos!,
ya que yo tengo que entregar mi rostro,
mi rostro, ¡mi rostro!, ¡ay, mi comido rostro!

These lines move from a concern with death, the consumptive blood on a handkerchief, to a concern with love and identity. The poet's face is consumed, like the gnawed breast of love earlier, and it seems as though love's extremities also are endangered. Love and identity are here equivalents.

The next stanza could well be read as a statement that the poet's anguished experience presented here is intended as an exemplar for the guidance of others similarly afflicted. The final stanza repeats the structure of stanza 4; there is no salvation, only the remembrance of lost childhood: "una cunita en el desván / que recuerda todas las cosas." Then as the insects appear clearly for the first time in the poem we are able to provide subjects for those third-person verbs of stanza 5 and also for the creatures which consume the poet's love and identity. But whereas stanza 4 ended with the exclamation "¡Mi amor!", this repetition ends with the emphatic statement of death as the only reality: "¡ ¡La luna!!"

This brief examination of some of the poems dealing with the city and the countryside has shown that they are not opposite but twin environments joined by the presence in both of an omnipotent, omnipresent death. The constant presence of an active death-force destroys the poet's innocence and love, and bears a large share of blame for the disturbance of his identity. Furthermore these poems reveal a strong metaphysical disquiet and a continual process of religious allusion which point to a failure of religious faith. This theme is made overt in two poems from "Calles y sueños" on the Nativity, poems which have been reserved for commentary in this study's next chapter.

IV The birth and Passion of Christ

A religious reference is a persistent feature of the New York poems;
we have already noted the continual negation of the term "cielo",
the emphasis on the spiritual, religious character of the Blacks, a
conflict between death and the possibility of religious consolation,
and a number of Christian allusions. These American poems are filled
both with a need for faith and with a sense of the failure of faith,
which is part of the poet's more general experience of disillusionment. The religious element of the book is made even stronger by a
number of poems that treat, more or less directly, the theme of
redemption presented by the birth and Passion of Christ. I shall
consider the poems in the order of their appearance in the book.

"Iglesia abandonada" is an enigmatic poem included rather strangely in the section "Los negros". The subtitle "Balada de la gran
guerra" probably reflects Lorca's reading of *All Quiet on the Western
Front* (*29*, p.35). This would also account for the allusions to war
and for the poem's structure as a father's lament for his dead son.
But the military frame of reference is subordinated to images of the
Mass and of the Passion. After the opening lines establish the poem
as a lament the dead son is mysteriously changed into a girl, then into
a fish:

> Comprendí que mi niña era un pez
> por donde se alejan las carretas.
> Yo tenía una niña.
> Yo tenía un pez muerto bajo las cenizas de los incensarios.

Perhaps it is the presence of death that creates the sexual ambivalence of the child. The change to a fish, normally an unpleasant
image in Lorca, may also be attributed to death, if "carretas" are
read in the sense of "tumbrils". The ashes in the censer acquire a
pejorative connotation, possibly an allusion to Ash Wednesday,
while it is tempting to see in "pez muerto" a negated form of the
traditional symbol for Christ. I interpret these lines to mean that
the presence of the dead son/daughter/fish continues to exist within,
and perhaps despite, the ritual of the Church which ought to be a

source of consolation for the father.

In the lines that follow there is a destructive conjunction of natural life-symbols and religious images, particularly the reference to the unlit candles of the church in Holy Week consuming the fertility symbol of corn. This oblique allusion to the Passion of Christ leads to a complex distortion of images of the Mass and the Nativity:

> En las anémonas del ofertorio te encontraré, ¡corazón mío!,
> cuando el sacerdote levante la mula y el buey con sus fuertes brazos,
> para espantar los sapos nocturnos que rondan los helados paisajes
> del cáliz.
> Yo tenía un hijo que era un gigante,
> pero los muertos son más fuertes y saben devorar pedazos de cielo.

The raised Host, transposed into images of the Birth, might be taken to suppress the menace symbolised in the toads around the chalice. However, the anemone in Christian symbology signifies death, while the ox and the mule can be read as sterile counterparts of the bull and the horse. The redemptive power of the Mass is further undermined by the image of the Host as pieces of sky/heaven, implying small and broken pieces of salvation. The hope of resurrection is devoured by the superior force of death. The Church, religious belief, has failed to provide the father with consolation for his son's death.

When the theme of the Mass returns towards the end of the poem the significance is rather cryptic. The father's breaking of the tiller could be an abandonment to grief, and by implication a despairing rejection of the Church, the barque of faith. A negative import is certainly implied by the madness of the penguins and the seagulls which negates their significance as life-symbols. The general pessimism I find in this poem can be seen clearly in the reference at the beginning to the moment of the son's death as "un viernes de todos los muertos". This fusion of Good Friday and All Souls' Day produces a concept by which I suggest Lorca seeks to deny both the singularity of the Crucifixion and the promise of resurrection contained in it. In his heterodox theology death is final and all powerful.

"Iglesia abandonada" is one of the more difficult of the New York poems. I interpret the poem as a statement of the loss of faith brought about by the experience of death, an interpretation supported by the negative intent of the title. The father's story could be a mask for Lorca's problems of faith, while the religious frame of reference itself might even be a mask for one of the basic concerns of *Poeta en Nueva York*, the loss of innocence. The dead child could then be Lorca's own former self; the reference at the poem's beginning to the child playing "en las últimas escaleras de la misa" could be an allusion to Lorca's childhood playacting at being a priest (*4*, p.16). It might even be possible that this is a lament by God the Father for His only-begotten Son, particularly when one considers the violently exclamatory anguish of the final lines.

A more open statement of the triumph of death over the Christian concept of redemption is made in "Navidad en el Hudson" from the section "Calles y sueños". This poem begins with an enumeration of negative elements, a grey sponge, a beheaded sailor, a breeze with restricting "límites oscuros", and love associated menacingly with the cutting edge of a knife. Then there appear four sailors struggling against the world of mechanistic values in New York. Given the religious context I suggest the four sailors are the Evangelists, subsequently multiplied by a surrealist caprice. The recently be-headed sailor who precedes them in the poem would thus be John the Baptist, while the "río grande" of the poem's third line would double as both the Hudson and the Jordan. The opening exclamation "¡Esa esponja gris!" becomes an obvious allusion to the Crucifixion.

The multitude of sailors are engaged in a futile struggle because "el mundo / estaba solo por el cielo", so the world can hope for no help from heaven. In the context of this poem "cielo" has lost its ambiguity. An even harsher statement, "el mundo solo por el cielo solo", stresses the hopelessness. Then, in the poem's third stanza, the celebration of the Nativity is mocked by a bitterly ironic use of the liturgical Hallelujah.

After this bleak declaration that the emptiness of heaven nullifies the promise of salvation in the Birth the poem's final stanza changes to a personal statement of a feeling of kinship with ordinary men, building workers, and of an involvement with the sailors' struggle to repair the damaged barque of faith. But the speaker's hands are empty and the Hudson continues to pour into the sea. The only thing of significance in New York is, paradoxically, the absence of all faith, the "hueco":

Lo que importa es esto: hueco. Mundo solo. Desembocadura.
Alba no. Fábula inerte.
Solo esto: desembocadura.

The dawn is here clearly the Light of the World, rendered empty and meaningless. The poem then concludes by repeating its opening lines now charged with an almost frenetic personal dimension. It is possible that the voice here belongs to Lorca himself, introducing an allusion to the sentimental crisis experienced before going to New York. But it seems more likely that the anguished exclamations come from Christ. The Nativity is linked with the Crucifixion via the image of the sponge and the images of pain and mutilation.

The lament for the impossibility of redemption is continued in "Nacimiento de Cristo", also in the section "Calles y sueños". Here a Crib is described surrounded by hostile elements and images of death:

Un pastor pide teta por la nieve que ondula
blancos perros tendidos entre linternas sordas.
El Cristito de barro se ha partido los dedos
en los filos eternos de la madera rota.

¡Ya vienen las hormigas y los pies ateridos!
Dos hilillos de sangre quiebran el cielo duro.

The snow locates the Crib in North America and also introduces an immediate negative note. The white dogs are a metamorphosis of the sheep, while "linternas sordas" make a synaesthetic sense-deprivation image out of the shepherds' lanterns. All of these negative images are presided over by a plea for sustenance. But the miniscule figurine of the Christ-Child has been injured, His fingers caught on a splinter of wood that foreshadows the Cross. The "filos eternos" repeat the image of the knife's cutting edge from "Navidad en el Hudson" together with an adjective that stresses the finality of death. Ants are a common negative symbol in the New York poems and the cold feet are an image of death. In another warped image of heaven, the Child's blood shatters the "cielo duro".

The weak, defenceless figure of the Infant Christ is in marked contrast to the powerful, hostile activity of the creatures around Him: wolves, the moon, a mutilated bull, and the same toads that roamed around the chalice in "Iglesia abandonada". The Child is already marked by death. Again the Crucifixion overshadows the Nativity. The three bronze thorns amongst the hay fuse the crown of thorns and the nails. The images of mutilation, stringless zithers and the decapitated voices of the massacred Innocents (*38*, p.99), and the "rumor de desierto" in the swaddling clothes, reveal that the Birth has produced no redemption from the eternal presence of death. This jaundiced version of the Nativity again laments the impotence of the Infant Christ. The Christmas message is once more seen as futile and meaningless in New York, like the idiot priests, imitation Cherubim and false ogives which conclude the poem.

The theme of the Crucifixion itself appears in a heavily disguised form in the poem "Vaca", from the fifth section of *Poeta en Nueva York*. While apparently a response to the sickness of a cow while Lorca was staying in Vermont (*16*, p.57), the poem contains an elaborate sequence of religious allusions. The cow in the poem has been killed, calling to mind the image of ritual sacrifice "la bovina cabeza recién cortada" from "Nocturno del hueco", and its blood stains the ambivalent sky/heaven, recalling the way the Infant Christ's blood shatters heaven in "Nacimiento de Cristo". In the fourth and sixth stanzas the poet requests that the cow's demise be reported to the symbols of death, roots and the moon, and also to a child sharpening a knife, whom I take as an ironic figure, the innocent about to butcher the corpse. The cow in "Vaca" is clearly presented as a sacrificial victim; in stanza 3 its death evokes a lament from the whole of the bovine kingdom, both living and dead. There are, moreover, a number of allusions to Christ. The line "rubor de luz o miel de establo" from stanza 3 could be taken to refer to the Nativity, while the "alarido blanco" in the second stanza could allude to the cry from the Cross and the Death of Christ.

Christ's death is presented undisguised in the poem entitled "Crucifixión", which Lorca intended to be the final poem of section VII (*12*, p.1). It opens with a violent image of sexual mutilation as the standard Lorcan death-symbol of the moon conflicts with the equally standard life-symbol of the horse. The moon has triumphed over life at the moment of the Crucifixion, which is made simultaneous with the ritual purification of the Circumcision, linking yet again the Birth and the Death of Christ. In Lorca's heterodoxy circumcision would, I suggest, be regarded as a sexual mutilation, performed here, significantly, on a dead child. The projection of the blood onto the sky/heaven repeats an image already seen in both

"Nacimiento de Cristo" and "Vaca".

The poem proceeds to examine the effects of the Crucifixion. The traditional motif of the angels' gathering of Christ's blood becomes in Lorca's version a failure because the chalices cannot contain it. The miracle of the Living Christ in the wine of the Mass will thus not be achieved, and there will be no Risen Christ. The strange presence of lame dogs smoking pipes is an image taken from an advertisement for an American tobacco company (*25*, p.512). Lorca has characteristically given the dogs a physical disability. An American background is also present in the people vomiting in the streets who recall "Paisaje de la multitud que vomita". At this point the association of the Crucifixion with sexual mutilation is reasserted: "Era que la luna quemaba con sus bujías el falo de los caballos."

There follows a sequence of specifically religious images all linked with the idea of death as inevitable and final. The three Marys are made to gaze upon a skull by a tailor specializing in the purple habit of the Holy Week penitent. A skull is a traditional attribute of Mary Magdalen, and also alludes to Golgotha. Christ himself, transformed quite logically for the purpose of this image into a camel, must pass through the eye of a needle. Here is a reference to the entry of Christ into the Kingdom of Heaven, although the biblical allusion makes an odd metaphor implying an unexpected degree of difficulty. This, together with the stressing of the inevitability of His death by the phrase "sin remedio", undermines the concept of redemption created by the Crucifixion. Immediately afterwards come the exclamations associated with the suffering on the Cross and the assertion that His death is for all eternity: " ¡Oh cruz! ¡Oh clavos! ¡Oh espina!/ ¡Oh espina clavada en el hueso hasta que se oxiden los planetas!"

The remainder of the poem's central section is designed to undermine the importance of the Crucifixion and stress that it was not a conquest of death. The Last Words from the Cross are degraded by the hostile pharisees, in a metamorphosis of the image of the camel, into the sound of a cow lowing because it has not been milked. The blood descending from the Cross is changed into rain determined to soak the hearts of the people, but they shut their doors against it, while the city dying with the fading of the Light is filled with the sounds of woodcutters and carpenters presumably making new crosses for the Christ rejected and thus recrucified. The pharisees then increase their denigration of the Crucified Christ, although at this point the poem makes a direct statement that the Crucifixion signifies the salvation of man: "Se supo el momento preciso de la salvación de nuestra vida." This, however, may be ironic, for immediately afterwards comes the curious image of the moon washing the burns it had earlier inflicted on the horse, reversing the moon's normally malignant role:

Porque la luna lavó con agua
las quemaduras de los caballos
y no la niña viva que callaron en la arena.

These lines have been interpreted as signifying the purification of sin by death (*25*, pp.521-2), but this is difficult to reconcile with the moon's act of sexual mutilation at the beginning of the poem. There is also a dubious assumption that sex for Lorca had any sinful connotations. A clear contrast exists in the lines between the moon and the "niña viva", who could well be a variant of the "niño muerto" of the opening lines and thus an image of Christ. Compare the hermaphrodite "hijo/niña" in "Iglesia abandonada". Marcilly interprets this passage to mean that death brings a salve for sexual mutilation but cannot harm the Living Christ, even though He is buried alive, i.e. ignored by the society He came to save (*25*, pp.521-2). However, it is more likely that "niña viva" is an alternative subject for "lavó", in which case the meaning would be that death brings release from the pain of life, not Christ in the Tomb, unrisen.

A deep sense of despair is also evident in the lines that lead to the poem's conclusion. The pharisees emphatically repeat their rejection of the Crucified Christ. As a result of His death the world is dominated by hostile elements symbolised as cold and frogs, recalling those toads of "Iglesia abandonada" and "Nacimiento de Cristo". The frogs' association with the fires along the river's banks is another product of the American locale —the lights of New York coming on at dusk along the Hudson. The crowds and the drunks again point to an American setting in which the pharisees desecrate the purity symbol of sacrificial salt, while ignoring the blood of the Slain Lamb. The poem ends with a final assertion of death's triumph in an allusion to the earth tremor and sudden darkness that accompanied Christ's death (*35*, p.228): "Fue entonces / y la tierra despertó arrojando temblorosos ríos de polilla."

Lorca's view of the Crucifixion is as gloomy as his view of the
Nativity; the death on the Cross is without the sure and certain hope
of the Resurrection.   The sacrifice is rendered impotent because
mankind rejects the promise of salvation. Thus what in the context
of "Danza de la muerte" he called "la muerte sin ángeles ni *resurrexit*"
reigns supreme.   Yet Lorca clearly laments what he regards as a
failure of the Coming. It might appear that his obsessive preoccupation with death stands in the way of an orthodox Christian belief
and that in his heterodox theology he finds it difficult to accept the
idea that a man must die to achieve salvation.

V A voice crying in the wilderness

On several occasions we have seen Lorca take on a prophetic voice, as for example in the vision of New York's destruction in "Danza de la muerte". I shall now examine three poems of denunciation where that voice acquires something of an Old Testament ring decrying the corruption of the world and, ultimately, preaching the coming of a new kingdom.

"New York. Oficina y denuncia", which begins the book's seventh section "Vuelta a la ciudad", is a condemnation of the city's lack of spirituality made in terms of almost stark clarity compared with the complicated diction of other poems. Lorca denounces the city's slaughter of millions of nature's creatures to sustain itself and the city's use of the blood of countless sacrificial victims to drive its machines and support the mathematics of its financial operations. This point is driven home by an obsessive repetition. Allusions to the theme of sacrifice can be seen in the image "sangre de marinero" of the poem's fourth line, which recalls the sailors of "Navidad en el Hudson", and also in the image towards the middle of the poem, "los terribles alaridos de las vacas estrujadas", which echoes other images of sacrificed cows while being more mundanely an emotionalisation of the sirens of ships on the Hudson. The phrase "el alba mentida de New York" from the ninth line and "los cielos hechos añicos" from line 23 recall respectively the corrupted dawn of "La aurora" and the many other images of a negated heaven.

After the initial statement of the devastation the city wreaks on nature the poet specifically rejects the possibility of averting his gaze from the scene to seek solace in the countryside, philosophy or heaven:

Existen las montañas, lo sé.
Y los anteojos para la sabiduría,
lo sé. Pero yo no he venido a ver el cielo.

He asserts categorically that his purpose is to confront the death the city promotes: "Yo he venido para ver la turbia sangre." Lorca's reaction to the destruction and corruption of nature has a directness and vehemence unequalled elsewhere in the book:

Yo denuncio a toda la gente
que ignora la otra mitad,
la mitad irredimible
que levanta sus montes de cemento
donde laten los corazones
de los animalitos que se olvidan
y donde caeremos todos
en la última fiesta de los taladros.
Os escupo en la cara.

Here is a social statement; the half of the people that are unaware of
the other half are the rich and powerful, while the other half are the
exploited who build the skyscrapers where are entombed the values
of nature. In such a situation all is death, seen again in the characteristic image of perforation. Lorca feels a solidarity with the exploited,
innocent half of the people: "La otra mitad me escucha / devorando,
cantando, volando, en su pureza / como los niños de las porterías."
Then come two lines that sum up in ringing tones the castigation of
New York: "No es el infierno, es la calle. / No es la muerte, es la
tienda de frutas."

The poem continues with further images of the destruction and
subjugation of nature. A cat's paw broken by a car is a small sign of
greater catastrophes, "ríos quebrados / y distancias inasibles". Little
girls have already in their hearts the worm their corpses will nourish.
All positive values are rendered absurd. Love will end in the grave, in
the photographs of the dead customarily found in Spanish cemeteries.
Lorca's response is an even more emphatic and rotund denunciation:

No, no; yo denuncio.
Yo denuncio la conjura
de estas desiertas oficinas
que no radian las agonías,
que borran los programas de la selva . . .

Here is a clear statement of the city's antagonism to nature, both
jamming the true voice of life and refusing to transmit the reality of
suffering and death. The poem concludes with Lorca offering himself as a sacrificial victim to those other victims of the city's blood-lust,
the crushed cows of the ships' sirens.

The social focus present in the denunciation of New York's
massacre of nature also appears strongly in "Grito hacia Roma", the
first of the two odes which form section VIII. It begins with a chaotic
enumeration of some very strange elements that ends with the phrase

"caerán sobre ti". This is the formula for a curse and the strange elements may thus be taken to have a noxious quality. Apples are a negative symbol, as are silver and the knife image "finos espadines". The clouds scratched by a coral hand are an image with an authentic surrealist ring, although the three opening lines could have quite rational links. The scratched clouds bring to mind the skyscrapers, topped with the "finos espadines" of radio aerials, while the apples become mutations of the clouds. The flaming almond on the back of the hand also seems a surrealist image, but I interpret this as a reference to the mandorla, the almond-shaped halo enclosing the figure of Christ at the Ascension. In early Christian art the mandorla was depicted as a cloud and later represented as an aureole of light. The figure of God the Father is frequently represented in art as a hand emerging from a cloud. The visual image of the "skyscraper" has thus been joined to some oblique religious references and the whole sequence of ideas dismembered and rearranged by a process of free association. The remaining elements of the curse are easier to identify as images of corruption, mutilation, violence and pain. All of these unpleasant things are to fall on the great dome, which in the context of Rome can only be that of St Peter's Basilica. Now we are dealing with a poem written not long after the signing of the Papal Concordat with Mussolini in February 1929. I suggest this is the reason for the curse being called down on the Church of Rome, a curse that includes, significantly, allusions to the wrath of God. The "lenguas militares" belong to the military agents of Fascism, who, in an image of caustic bitterness, are seen giving the Sacrament of Extreme Unction to the Church. The result of this unholy alliance is that the function of the Church has been totally degraded. The white Host of the Mass, the symbol of the Resurrected Body of Christ, is spat out as chewed coal, recalling the pharisees spitting out of the sacrificial salt in "Crucifixión". The unidentified man, soon to be revealed as Pius XI, urinates on the shining dove, a traditional symbol of the Holy Ghost.

The ode's second stanza emphatically declares that the Church has lost its power to console through the Mass, and in particular its power to offer salvation from death. The phrase "los linos del reposo" alludes to the Raising of Lazarus and is thus an image of the Resurrection. The wounded elephants are yet another use of animals

in the Zoo to symbolise suffering. There will be no redemption, un-
born children have chains awaiting them and carpenters make coffins
without crosses, the symbol of resurrection. The man who desecrated
the dove is indirectly ordered to abase himself amongst the columns
of the Basilica, to become a leper and to wash away with his tears
the material possessions of the Church. The stanza concludes with a
crushing indictment:

> Pero el hombre vestido de blanco
> ignora el misterio de la espiga,
> ignora el gemido de la parturienta,
> ignora que Cristo puede dar agua todavía,
> ignora que la moneda quema el beso de prodigio
> y da la sangre del cordero al pico idiota del faisán.

Here the anonymous man is clearly identified as the Pope by his
white clothes, a now ironic symbol of purity. The Pope, who has
just received an injunction to return to the true message of Christ, to
aid the poor and the suffering, is now declared to be unaware of
humanity's plight. Fertility symbols, the ear of the corn and the
woman in labour, are mingled with Christian references, the kiss of
peace of the Mass and the Blood of the Lamb. This is a castigation of
the Church for allowing materialism to vitiate its consoling function,
yet nonetheless there is an unequivocal statement here that Christ is
still the source of the Water of Life.

The attack on the Church continues unabated in the third stanza.
What should have been the marvellous light descended from the
mount is declared to have turned into "una reunión de cloacas /
donde gritan las oscuras ninfas del cólera". The Church is seen as
empty of love; the statues' eyes are made of "cristal definitivo", the
same image of glass used elsewhere as a death-symbol here linked to
the characteristic Lorcan association of death with blindness. Real
love, by implication the love of Christ, is to be found in the suffering
of mankind, a suffering that includes the pain of sexual frustration:
"el oscurísimo beso punzante   debajo de las almohadas." But the
Pope, now transformed into "el viejo de las manos traslúcidas" and
surrounded by suffering humanity, "el tisú estremecido de ternura",
continues to preach the Church's empty doctrine to the acclaim of
"millones de moribundos" who will not be redeemed from death. In
the midst of a political and social circumstance on the point of ex-
plosion, "el tirite de cuchillos y melones de dinamita", the Pope will

ironically preach peace until he himself dies and his lips turn to silver in an allusion to the coins placed on the eyes and mouths of the dead.

The poem concludes with a declaration that in view of the Church's corruption and impotence the oppressed victims of society must seek their own salvation. The people who work with their hands, their emotions or their imagination, "la muchedumbre de martillo, de violín o de nube", must rise up against the Church and the city that supports the Church, shouting seven times, in an allusion to Joshua circling the walls of Jericho, until the structure of the Church and the city comes tumbling down. The biblical allusion prepares for the final lines that parody the Lord's Prayer, turning it into a prayer for the will of the Earth to be done, that same Earth referred to at the end of "Panorama ciego de Nueva York" as the only reality for man. This prayer links an image of nature, "flor de aliso", with human suffering, "perenne ternura desgranada", in a desire for an embrace with nature which will bring to man the consolation the Church cannot provide. His daily bread will come from Earth, not Heaven, as a product of the "misterio de la espiga", offering an alternative set of ethical values to those the Church has corrupted.

Lorca's attack on the 1929 Concordat is made from the standpoint of an outraged believer; Pius XI is, in his view, no different from the pharisees who reject the Crucified Christ. However, he is not content with just expressing outrage, but proposes a personal, and religiously unorthodox, solution of a return to a form of primitive Christianity in which the institutionalised Church is abandoned in favour of a pantheistic communion with the natural world. The vehemence of "Grito hacia Roma" is as strong as in "New York. Oficina y denuncia", and despite the religious context the social concern is perhaps even more direct. The first of the odes is a remarkable poem, remarkable for the violence of its anticlericalism in a literature that has a strong tradition of such sentiments, and remarkable for its political reference which is the only case I know in Lorca's work of an allusion to a contemporary political event. Yet the second of the odes is no less remarkable, but for different reasons.

The "Oda a Walt Whitman" is focussed on an unconventional

aspect of the poet of *Leaves of Grass*, not Whitman the voice of
America but Whitman the homosexual. The ode begins by deftly
evoking the urban, industrial world juxtaposed with an overtly homosexual erotic image: "los muchachos cantaban enseñando sus cintu-
ras, / con la rueda, el aceite, el cuero y el martillo." The second
stanza clearly states that in this environment no-one sleeps, and by
implication no-one dreams of a communion with nature, of becoming
one with river, plant and sea. The following stanza begins with a
reprise of the opening lines, plus images of the loss of sexual innocence
and of the opposition between the city and nature:

> y los judíos vendían al fauno del río
> la rosa de la circuncisión
> y el cielo desemboca por los puentes y los tejados
> manadas de bisontes empujadas por el viento.

New York was and is the largest Jewish city in the world, something
that would have been particularly striking for a Spaniard, since the
Jewish population of Spain is almost non-existent. The Jewish
purification rite of circumcision is associated through the colour of
blood with the erotic symbol of the rose. The Jews' selling of "la
rosa de la circuncisión" is an act of base treachery, an act of corruption with specifically sexual overtones. The presence of the faun
also has sexual associations, but I interpret this classical allusion in
a negative way, linking the faun with the hostile nymphs we have
seen elsewhere. A similar corrupting association with the city can be
seen in the sky/heaven whose clouds have been brought down to the
level of the roof-tops and the bridges, while being transformed aptly
into herds of bison fleeing before the wind, recalling the image of
clouds as camels in "Norma y paraíso de los negros".

The fourth stanza is a parallel to the second, listing images of
nature and images that are rejected by the inhabitants of the city.
The pattern of the poem is then broken by the threatened appearance
of the moon, which will bring down the sky/heaven as though it
were a piece of stage scenery, while on a human level producing
pain and violence. This opening section of the ode is completed in
the sixth stanza by a statement of New York's corruption where the
"anémonas manchadas", another image of defiled blood, are contrasted with the fertility symbols of nature, "las verdades del trigo".

The seventh stanza begins an apostrophe to Whitman, the first

time he has been mentioned in the poem. The American poet is
identified with the natural world, "tu barba llena de mariposas . . .
anciano hermoso como la niebla", and he is seen as a paragon of manly
beauty. But the reference to him as an "Apolo virginal" is calculated
to desexualise him. He is also described as "enemigo del sátiro, /
enemigo de la vid", evoking dyonisian images that conflict with the
apollonian cult of chastity. Here one can see the reason for the
earlier allusion to the faun. Whitman is also associated with an
image of acute sexual frustration, "gemías igual que un pájaro / con
el sexo atravesado por una aguja". But above all he is seen as having
remained aloof from the contamination of the industrialised world,
and so to have been able to dream the dream alluded to in stanzas 2
and 4:

> soñabas ser un río y dormir como un río
> con aquel camarada que pondría en tu pecho
> un pequeño dolor de ignorante leopardo.

The dream is now revealed as specifically sexual and homosexual,
but the sexual experience has been transformed, almost transcended,
into a communion of innocence with the elemental life-force of
nature.

Whitman's transcendent view of sexuality is then contrasted with
the homosexual demi-monde whose inhabitants try to corrupt the
purity of Whitman's love. Lorca is here making a clear ethical
distinction between Whitman's spiritual, pantheistic homosexual
love and the debased sexuality of the "maricas". The moral tone
becomes particularly marked as the poem proceeds to its close.
After a reassertion of the ideal of love in stanza 12 there occurs a
phrase with a clear biblical resonance: "Porque es justo que el hombre
no busque su deleite / en la selva de sangre de la mañana próxima."
This statement of sexual restraint is balanced in the following stanza
by a denunciation of the rottenness of the world where all is death
and the ideal cannot exist, "y la vida no es noble, ni buena, ni sagra-
da". Stanza 15 returns to the tone of moral inquiry, contrasting
the apollonian "celeste desnudo" with its dyonisian counterpart
"vena de coral", both subject to and nullified by time.

The following stanza is linked causally with this idea. Lorca
refuses to denounce sexual frustration presented in a sequence of
both homosexual and heterosexual images, then turns with new fury

to his attack on the "maricas".

The ode's final stanza comes back to the address to Whitman, firstly advising him to sleep on since there is nothing left of his America, and then expressing a wish for his resurrection:

Quiero que el aire fuerte de la noche más honda
quite flores y letras del arco donde duermes
y un niño negro anuncie a los blancos del oro
la llegada del reino de la espiga.

The "arco" alludes to the cemetery niche from which Lorca wishes the wreath and the inscription to be removed as Whitman is raised from the dead at the coming of an earthly kingdom. Significantly it is a black child, a doubly innocent image, who will bring to the materialist whites the good news of the triumph of the pantheistic life-force, that same "misterio de la espiga" ignored by the Pope in "Grito hacia Roma".

VI Coda: three dances

Poeta en Nueva York reaches an emotional climax in the powerful denunciations and declarations of the odes to Rome and Whitman. The book's final two sections comprise just three fairly short poems which have a lessened emotional intensity and may be regarded as forming a coda to the collection. These last poems are also linked by their reference to dance forms. The two waltzes that are the vehicle for Lorca's "Huida de Nueva York" in the ninth section allude to the culture of the old world; the section has the subtitle "Dos valses hacia la civilización". But by 1930 the waltz was no longer in fashion; the Black Bottom was the dance of the moment. Moreover, European society had changed fundamentally since the days of Strauss's Vienna. Lorca's "Pequeño vals vienés" is not what might be expected from the title.

The poem utilises some popular song techniques, a refrain repeated with variants and a listing of disparate elements. It also uses a process of triple repetition and sequences of three images to give an impression of the 3/4 time of the dance. The assonantal rhyme scheme employs the unusual feature of monorhyme, affecting five lines in stanza 4 and the whole of the first stanza with the single, significant, exception of the word "muerte" in the second line. The repeated rhyme replaces the swirling rhythm of the waltz with a sense of monotony.

The enumerated elements of the first stanza contain images of death and of the degradation of nature: "palomas disecadas . . . un fragmento de la mañana / en el museo de la escarcha." The sombre note is reinforced by a quadruple " ¡Ay!" of lament, and by the final line, which forms the refrain: "Toma este vals con la boca cerrada." The image of the shut mouth implies a state less than rapture. The Viennese waltz would seem to have become for Lorca another version of the dance of death. The three-line second stanza stresses the ambivalence of the dance: "este vals / de sí, de muerte y de coñac / que moja su cola en el mar." The "sí" and the "coñac", allusions to the romantic connotations of the waltz, are set starkly against the mention of death, while the long ball-gown of the dancer is animalised into a tail, undermining the elegance of the dance.

The poem's eroticism becomes more assertive in the last three stanzas, although always appearing in company with images of repression and death. In stanza 4 the pun "muerte para piano" (a variation of "sonata para piano"), which negates the waltz's associations of cultural refinement, is linked with a characteristic Lorcan image of sexual repression, boys painted blue, the ethical colour of sterility. This leads to a reference to beggars and to "frescas guirnaldas de llanto" where "guirnalda" is clearly being used in its meaning of wreath. The variant in the refrain, "este vals que se muere en mis brazos", emphasises the presence of death in the erotic context, while being on an immediate level an allusion to the dancer swaying rapturously in her partner's arms.

The fifth stanza returns to images of nostalgia, "desván . . . soñando viejas luces de Hungría . . . tarde tibia", but these merge into more oppressive references to the negative colour white, "ovejas y lirios de nieve", and to repression or death, "el silencio oscuro de tu frente". The concluding stanza contains a rich mixture of ambivalent images of death and eroticism. It opens with an allusion to a masked ball, but the mask the poet promises to wear will be "un disfraz que tenga / cabeza de río", fusing the human presence with a forceful image of nature. However, the idea of "disfraz" introduces an element of falsification and perhaps another glimpse of the personality problem seen elsewhere. The narcissistic image at the beginning of stanza 4, "hay cuatro espejos / donde juegan tu boca y los ecos", could also be significant in this context. The fifth and sixth lines refer to a division of the body from the soul: "Dejaré mi boca entre tus piernas, / mi alma en fotografías y azucenas." The body is represented by a strikingly overt sexual image, while the lilies and the photographs are a reference to death. The soul will thus receive a quietus while the body is celebrated. The river imagery of the stanza leads to the final idea of the poet drowning in the dark waters of the object of his desire whose sinuous movements are like waves:

y en las ondas oscuras de tu andar
quiero, amor mío, dejar,
violín y sepulcro, las cintas del vals.

The waltz's romantic associations, the violin, are linked directly with death, but this dance of death is left for the metaphorical death of abandonment in love. This seems to bring the poem to a subdued climax, although the final dance with the lover will take place in Vienna, and from the evidence of the poem that is a city to be avoided.

"Vals en las ramas" changes to the more mundane frame of reference of children's song, combining the techniques of a counting game with those of a nonsense rhyme. The opening allusion to elegiac autumn leaves is offset by the song mode, although the fourth line, "Por la luna nadaba un pez", which in the song convention would be a nonsense element, introduces in Lorca's private convention an image of great menace. But the poem continues on its apparently childish way. The arbitrariness of lines 5 and 6 introduces a sequence of lines whose content is largely dictated by rhyme, although the idea of "La dama ... muerta en la rama" does add another note of menace. The seemingly innocent song is then interrupted by a further elegiac reference:

> Pero el ruiseñor
> lloraba sus heridas alrededor.
> Y yo también
> porque cayó una hoja ...

Here the nightingale which traditionally sings a song of lost love might also be assumed to be suffering from physical wounds. Note too that the voice of the poet identifies itself with the elegy. There then follow three lines that are more disturbing than arbitrary:

> Y una cabeza de cristal
> y un violín de papel
> y la nieve podría con el mundo ...

A glass head and a paper violin are both denatured objects no longer capable of serving their proper function, while the negative image of snow dominates the world.

At this point the children's song convention is disrupted by two highly emotional exclamations: " ¡Oh duro marfil de carnes invisibles! / ¡Oh golfo sin hormigas del amanecer!" This is the language of lament to be expected in a much more formal elegy. I take the first exclamation to be a reference to the dead. As for the second, ants in the New York poems tend to have a strongly negative significance.

A dawn without ants would therefore be positive and I suggest that this is an image of paradise, beyond the grave.

The poem then returns to the nonsense technique but this is further interrupted by a darker series of images. The reference to the crown of laurels should not be taken as a positive image of victory. As well as being associated with poets the laurel was also in antiquity an attribute of Apollo and sacred to the Vestal Virgins. It is therefore a symbol of chastity. Furthermore the laurel crowns only a torso, a body whose substance is reduced even more by being made of shadow. This is an image of death, which leads smoothly into yet another negation of the sky/heaven. The "él" with whom the fallen leaves dance away I take to be the torso now linked with the death-symbol of the moon in a return to the poem's opening lines. Although the reference to the moon is followed by a parallel line, "alrededor del sol", the poem's final image is of death's permanence: "para que los marfiles se duerman bien". All through this waltz there is a deliberate ambivalence between the popular framework and the personal emotional charge this is made to carry. The use of children's song techniques provides a method of understating a weighty theme for ironic effect, as the light, bantering form becomes a vehicle for a pessimistic meditation on decay and death. This children's waltz is another dance of death.

Poeta en Nueva York's concluding poem changes to the entirely American rhythm of a Cuban dance. In his 1932 lecture on his American experiences Lorca presents Cuba as a tropical transposition of his native Andalusia, a place with a vital folk culture which he tried to capture in his own "son". He also describes the island as "la América con raíces, la América de Dios" (*1*, I, p.1103). Lorca's "son" must be seen in the context of the poems about the Blacks of New York, since he clearly regarded the Cuban Black, like his northern brother, as retaining a close contact with a spiritual life-force.

The opening line, however, immediately evokes the death image of the moon, although it is not clear whether Santiago is a place of escape from death or somewhere associated with death. An element of menace is certainly present in the image "un coche de aguas negras" which combines an allusion to a hearse with a negation of the positive symbol of water. The eighth and tenth lines introduce the theme of metamorphosis: the palm tree wishes to change into a stork while the banana tree wants to become a jelly-fish ("plátano" and "medusa" are ambiguous but I suggest these are the most likely meanings here). The trees wish to change into a creature of the air and a creature of the sea, thus to lose their terrestrial form. This seems very much like an image of escape, and escape perhaps from death, which might point to Santiago being a refuge from death.

There follows a series of allusions to Lorca's childhood presented in almost perversely oblique references to Cuban cigars. "La rubia cabeza de Fonseca" alludes to the portrait of the gentleman of that name on the underside of the lid of the box containing the Havana cigars Lorca's father smoked. "El rosa de Romeo y Julieta" refers to the pink-coloured picture on the same box of Shakespeare's hero and heroine whose names have been borrowed for one of the most famous types of Cuban cigar. The "mar de papel y plata de monedas" refers again to the box and specifically to the medals won as prizes by the cigar company. These images are thus most apt within a Cuban context, although they had gone unrecognised until pointed out by a Cuban (*11*, p.18). Yet these are more than local allusions, they are a memory of childhood that links the poet's discovery of Cuba with the secure world of his early years.

The poem then moves on to a sequence of seemingly eulogistic exclamations addressed to Cuba. There is, however, a possibly sombre undertone in some of the images. The rhythm of the maracas is produced by "semillas secas"; behind the literal reference lies the metaphorical meaning of "dead" seeds. "Cintura caliente" evokes the vitality of the dance amidst the sound of the orchestra's Cuban percussion instruments, "gota de madera". But then two positive nature images appear with a cayman, the American crocodile closely associated with death in the poems written in New York: " ¡Arpa de troncos vivos, caimán, flor de tabaco!" Lorca has explained that the line "mi coral en la tiniebla" refers to a cigar-end glowing in the darkness (*3*, p.453). The maritime associations of coral link with the line "El mar ahogado en la arena", which appears innocent enough —sea soaking into the sand— until the forcefulness of the term "ahogado" brings out the symbolic meaning of the sea as a life-force. Moreover, sand is used by Lorca as a negative image. The next line has two staccato examples of destructive adjectivisation: "muerta"

negates "fruta", and I suggest that "blanco" has the same effect on
"calor". The positive meaning of heat is negated by white as the
ethical colour of sterility in Lorca's symbol system. These negative
notes affect even the final exclamation " ¡Oh bovino frescor de
cañavera!", since elsewhere we have seen the adjective "bovino", or
the noun "vaca", associated with sacrificial victims. The "Son de
negros en Cuba" is not entirely a celebration of Caribbean vitality.
Just as in the two waltz poems, beneath the dance runs the counter-
rhythm of the dance of death. The final poem of *Poeta en Nueva
York* is not a triumphant reassertion of Hispanic values but a dying
fall, a reassertion of the "ímpetu primitivo", the old force of death.

VII Conclusion

This study has concentrated on an analysis of the meaning of the poems of *Poeta en Nueva York* in as much detail as limited space would allow. The poems' difficulty makes this a primary concern. I hope to have shown that Lorca's American book is not merely a record of his experiences in the New World. The fundamental subject of the book is the poet not the city. New York provides an alternative backdrop against which to examine the obsessional themes of life and death, love and sterility. But *Poeta en Nueva York* is not an exotic variation on themes already familiar from Lorca's Andalusian poems. Familiar themes are presented with a greater clarity which illuminates earlier usage, and Lorca's system of values also becomes more fully elaborated. The ethical and religious condemnation of the city is joined with a social and essentially political denunciation. Lorca's private preoccupations, especially sexual and religious ones, are likewise present in a less equivocal fashion than elsewhere.

The book is, however, not only significant for the light it throws on Lorca's other work. I have suggested repeatedly that behind these poems there is a crisis of identity, but it is a crisis that the poems themselves resolve. As Angel del Río has declared: "Se puede decir que el poeta se encontró a sí mismo en Nueva York, o, al menos, que descubrió aquí algunas nuevas capas de su más íntima personalidad" (*29*, p.14). It could be said that Lorca reaches his maturity in *Poeta en Nueva York*. Yet the really outstanding achievement of these poems is the creation of an original and powerful language. Lorca takes the freedom of image formation developed by surrealism and utilises this to produce a means of expression of great richness, immense subtlety and enormous emotional power. The emotive force of these poems and their intellectual message have an intensity unrivalled anywhere in Lorca's work. Such is the power and importance of *Poeta en Nueva York*, and so forcefully does it state Lorca's view of the world, that I believe it should be regarded not, as is sometimes the case, as an aberration in the flow of Spanish-inspired

poems and plays, but as the central element of the Lorcan canon,
the work by which all others should be judged.

Bibliographical Note

This bibliography lists only works that have been found useful in the preparation of this guide. For additional bibliography see the edition of Lorca's *Obras completas* listed below, also J. L. Laurenti and J. Siracusa, *Federico García Lorca y su mundo. Ensayo de una bibliografía general* (Metuchen, N.J.: The Scarecrow Press, 1974).

Editions
1. Federico García Lorca, *Obras completas*, 19th edition (Madrid: Aguilar, 1974).

2. —, '*Trip to the Moon*: A Filmscript', *New Directions*, 18 (1964), 33-41.

Textual problems and biography
3. Auclair, Marcelle, *Enfances et mort de García Lorca* (Paris: Editions du Seuil, 1968). An extensive biography particularly useful for detailed information on "Son de negros en Cuba".

4. Cano, José Luis, *García Lorca. Biografía ilustrada* (Barcelona: Destino, 1962). A brief but very sound biography.

5. Eisenberg, Daniel, 'Dos textos primitivos de *Poeta en Nueva York*', *Papeles de Son Armadans*, LXXIV (1974), 169-71. Early versions of the poems "El niño Stanton" and "Cielo vivo".

6. —, *Textos y documentos lorquianos* (Tallahassee: Florida State University, 1975). Contains an account of a lecture on folk song given by Lorca at Vassar College in 1930.

7. —, 'Cuatro pesquisas lorquianas', *Thesaurus*, XXX (1975), 1-19. Extremely interesting information concerning Lorca's residence in Columbia University and also the poem "El niño Stanton".

8. —, 'Dos conferencias lorquianas (Nueva York y La Habana, 1930)', *Papeles de Son Armadans*, LXXIX (1975), 197-212. Two variant versions of the lecture "Imaginación, inspiración, evasión", originally given by Lorca in Granada in 1928.

9. —, ed., Federico García Lorca, *Songs* (Pittsburgh: Duquesne University Press, 1976). Contains much useful information about Lorca's stay in Vermont.

10. —, '*Poeta en Nueva York*'. *Historia y problemas de un texto de Lorca* (Barcelona: Ariel, 1976). A major contribution towards unravelling the textual problems of *Poeta en Nueva York*.

11. Marinello, Juan, *García Lorca en Cuba* (Havana: Ediciones Especiales, 1965). Reproduces early versions of "Poema doble del lago Edem" and "Son de negros en Cuba". Detailed information about the latter poem is particularly useful.

12. Martín, Eutimio, '¿Existe una versión definitiva de *Poeta en Nueva York*, de Lorca?', *Insula*, 310 (September 1972), 1 and 10. An examination of the textual problems of the book.

13. —, '*Tierra y luna*: ¿un libro adscrito abusivamente a *Poeta en Nueva York*?', *Trece de nieve*, 1-2 (December 1976), 125-31. An examination of the problems of structure and content of the book.

14. Martínez Nadal, Rafael, *Federico García Lorca. Autógrafos* (Oxford: Dolphin, 1975). Reproduces manuscript versions of "Oda a Walt Whitman" and "Oda al rey de Harlem".

15. Paepe, Christian de, 'García Lorca: posiciones, oposiciones, proposiciones y contraposiciones (Apostillas a la documentación lorquiana)', *Cuadernos Hispanoamericanos*, XC (1972), 271-99. A survey of textual problems.

16. Schwartz, Kessel, 'Lorca and Vermont', in *The Meaning of Existence in Contemporary Hispanic Literature* (Coral Gables: University of Miami, 1969), pp. 52-61. Provides useful details concerning the poems written in Vermont, especially "Vaca" and "Cielo vivo".

Works on Poeta en Nueva York

17. Allen, Rupert Jr., 'Una explicación simbológica de "Iglesia abandonada" de Lorca', *Hispanófila*, 26 (January 1966), 33-44. A Jungian analysis.

18. Craige, Betty Jean, *Lorca's 'Poeta en Nueva York'. The Fall into Consciousness* (Studies in Romance Languages, XV, Lexington: University Press of Kentucky, 1977). A Jungian analysis, particularly perceptive about the book's structure.

19. Díaz-Plaja, Guillermo, 'García Lorca y su Nueva York', *Luz* (Madrid), 28-XII-32, p.3. An early commentary notable for insights into the nature of the poems' expression.

20. Harris, Derek, 'A la caza de la imagen surrealista en Lorca', *Insula*, 368-9 (July-August 1977), 19. An analysis of image-building techniques.

21. —, 'The Religious Theme in Lorca's *Poeta en Nueva York*', *Bulletin of Hispanic Studies*, LIV (1977), 315-26. A commentary on "Iglesia abandonada", "Navidad en el Hudson", "Nacimiento de Cristo", "Crucifixión" and "Grito hacia Roma".

22. Higginbotham, Virginia, 'Reflejos de Lautréamont en *Poeta en Nueva York*', *Hispanófila*, 46 (September 1972), 59-68. In addition to the interesting comparative element there is perceptive commentary on the poetic mode of *Poeta en Nueva York*.

23. López Landeira, Richard, 'Un puente entre dos puentes', *Revista Hispánica Moderna*, XXXV (1969), 261-7. A comparison of "Ciudad sin sueño" and Mayakovsky's poem "Brooklyn Bridge".

24. Marcilly, C., *Ronde et fable de la solitude à New York* (Paris: Ediciones Hispano-Americanas, 1962). A detailed and impressively penetrating reading of the first five poems of the book.

25. —, 'Notes pour l'étude de la pensée religieuse de F. García Lorca: "Crucifixión"', *Bulletin Hispanique*, LXIV bis (1962: *Mélanges offerts à Marcel Bataillon*), 507-25. A detailed and enormously perceptive analysis of the poem.

26. Menarini, Piero, *'Poeta en Nueva York' di Federico García Lorca: lettura critica* (Florence: La Nuova Italia, 1975). A marxist-oriented thematic study.

27. Ortega, Julio, 'García Lorca, poeta social: "los negros" (*Poeta en Nueva York*)', *Cuadernos Hispanoamericanos*, CVII (1977), 407-19. A thematic commentary on the role of the Blacks.

28. Predmore, Richard L., 'New York y la conciencia social de Federico García Lorca', *Revista Hispánica Moderna*, XXXVI (1970-71), 32-40. A survey of the social dimension of the poems.

29. Río, Angel del, *García Lorca: 'Poeta en Nueva York'* (Madrid: Gredos, 1958). A fundamental work giving much important biographical detail.

30. Saez, Richard, 'Ritual Sacrifice in Lorca's *Poeta en Nueva York*', in *Lorca. A Collection of Critical Essays*, ed. by Manuel Durán (Englewood Cliffs, N.J.: Prentice Hall, 1962), pp. 108-29. An interesting comparison of *Poeta en Nueva York* and Eliot's *The Waste Land*.

31. Vidal, Hernán, '"Paisaje de la multitud que vomita": poema de ruptura de la visión mítica en García Lorca', *Romance Notes*, X (1968-69), 226-32. An analysis of the poem from the point of view of its relationship to a mythic view of the world.

General works

32. Correa, Gustavo, *La poesía mítica de Federico García Lorca* (Madrid: Gredos, 1970). A fundamental work particularly illuminating about Lorca's use of symbols.

33. Feal Deibe, Carlos, *Eros y Lorca* (Barcelona: Edhasa, 1973). A mainly Freudian analysis of the *Romancero gitano* which provides, incidentally, much detailed information about Lorca's use of symbols.

34. Fusero, Clemente, *García Lorca* (Milan: dall'Oglio, 1969). A general survey, in Italian, of Lorca's life and work. *Poeta en Nueva York* is linked perceptively with the expressionist mode.

35. Laffranque, Marie, *Les Idées esthétiques de Federico García Lorca*

(Paris: Centre de Recherches Hispaniques, 1967). A searching analysis of the development of Lorca's literary theory, and the best book on him to date.

36. —, 'Puertas abiertas y cerradas en la poesía y el teatro de Federico García Lorca', in *Federico García Lorca*, ed, by I. M. Gil (Madrid: Taurus, 1973), pp. 249-69. A wide-ranging article that contains interesting comments on "Grito hacia Roma", "Iglesia abandonada" and "Oda a Walt Whitman".

37. Morris, C. B., *Surrealism and Spain* (Cambridge: University Press, 1972). A detailed and fundamental history of the development of surrealism in Spain.

38. Onís, Carlos Marcial de, *El surrealismo y cuatro poetas de la generación del 27* (Madrid: José Porrúa Turanzas, 1974). A general but very sound survey of the influence of surrealism on Lorca, Luis Cernuda, Rafael Alberti and Vicente Aleixandre.

39. Ory, Carlos Edmundo de, *Lorca* (Paris: Editions Universitaires, 1967). A short but very useful introduction to Lorca by a poet from the post-Civil War period who has himself been influenced by surrealism.

40. Ramos-Gil, Carlos, *Claves líricas de García Lorca* (Madrid: Aguilar, 1967). A wide-ranging and perceptive analysis of the diction of Lorca's poetry that makes frequent reference to *Poeta en Nueva York*.

41. Vázquez Ocaña, Fernando, *García Lorca. Vida, cántico y muerte* (Mexico City: Gandesa, 1957). A general survey of Lorca's life and work which perceptively notes the expressionistic manner of *Poeta en Nueva York*.